Wakefield Press

MARGARET & DAVID

5 Stars

MARGARET & DAVID

major essay by
Sandy George

with contributions from

Geoffrey Rush, Fred Schepisi, Jan Chapman, Cate Shortland,
Gillian Armstrong, Andrew Bovell, Josh Pomeranz, Al Clark,
Richard Kuipers, Jay Weatherill, Andrew Mackie,
Sandra Levy, Nashen Moodley, Adolfo Aranjuez,
Kath Shelper and Warwick Thornton

edited by
Amanda Duthie

**Wakefield
Press**

Wakefield Press
16 Rose Street
Mile End
South Australia 5031
www.wakefieldpress.com.au

First published 2017

Edited by Julia Beaven, Wakefield Press
Cover designed by Liz Nicholson, designBITE
Text designed and typeset by Michael Deves, Wakefield Press

ISBN 978 1 74305 513 7

A catalogue record for this book is available from the National Library of Australia

contents

foreword

Sandra Sdraulig, AM
Chair, Adelaide Film Festival

The Don Dunstan Award was initiated by the Adelaide Film Festival in honour of the late Don Dunstan, Premier of South Australia from 1967 to 1968 and 1970 to 1979.

Dunstan's visionary commitment to the arts led to the establishment of various cultural organisations including the South Australian Film Corporation.

The Don Dunstan Award is presented by the Board of the Adelaide Film Festival in recognition of the outstanding contribution by individuals who, through their work, have significantly enriched Australian screen culture.

In 2017, the Adelaide Film Festival Board honours the extraordinary contribution from two leading lights of Australian screen culture, Margaret Pomeranz and David Stratton.

Margaret and David have been the Patrons of the Adelaide Film Festival since 2013 and we have welcomed them back to South Australia for every event. Their passion for cinema is greatly appreciated by audiences and by industry alike. It's been an absolute honour to work with them to enhance and promote screen culture in Australia.

Previous recipients:

2003   actor David Gulpilil

2005   documentary filmmaker Dennis O'Rourke

2007   writer/director Rolf de Heer

2009   producer Jan Chapman

2011   actor Judy Davis

2013   writer/director Scott Hicks

2015   writer Andrew Bovell

I would like to acknowledge the invaluable support of Arts SA who made this production possible, and Wakefield Press for their commitment to the project.

Fred Schepisi, AO

has worked as a highly successful award-winning director,
writer and producer in Australia and the US.
As a director, his films include *The Devil's Playground,*
Evil Angels, Six Degrees of Separation and
The Eye of the Storm.

introduction

Fred Schepisi

How fortunate we Aussie filmmakers are to have two such champions for our movies.

Margaret and David are critics who love movies to the point of obsession – fortunately, for all the right reasons. Ever ready to praise yet not afraid to give criticism, while ensuring it's constructive; looking more for the chance to encourage than damn. These are qualities helpful to us moviemakers, even more helpful in attracting audiences, and educating these audiences how to watch our movies. How to appreciate the finer points, the subtexts and cultural overtones, the achievements, originality and boldness. How to put into perspective the creative attempts that may not quite have hit their mark, maybe through inexperience, maybe through eagerness to experiment, to push the boundaries, find the Australian way, the Australian voice for our cinema and put that into perspective with world cinema. Not just Hollywood but the whole world. Margaret and David always consider the larger picture. Theirs is a fountain of knowledge to be drawn from with relish. Often opinionated, never elitist, even their disagreements were wonderfully informative, challenging and rarely dismissive. Australian cinema is all the better for their engagement and Australian moviemakers owe them a great debt.

Cate Shortland

has written and directed award-winning short films
Pentuphouse, Flowergirl and *Joy*, and feature films *Somersault,
Lore* and *The Berlin Syndrome*. Her television directing includes
The Secret Life of Us and *The Silence* and her TV writing includes
Rosie, adapted from a chapter in Christos Tsiolkas' novel
The Slap, and episodes for miniseries *The Devil's Playground,
Gallipoli* and *The Kettering Incident*.

[Photo: Adam Arkapow]

creating a space

Cate Shortland

Before I was a filmmaker I was a teenage fan. Sitting next to the Vulcan bar heater in a suburban house watching *The Movie Show*. Listening to people speak about ideas, story, nuance, about beauty. How we all connect through story. It was part of my inkling that cinema was important. That films don't have to please us but somehow make us think. That easy is not always best. And that an animation or a documentary can be as mind-blowing as a drama.

How incredible in Australia in the 1990s to witness a woman debating publicly with a man and being heard. Margaret's ideas mattered and she had a public voice in a time when we were often silenced. Thank you both for creating that space.

You made us feel part of it, your intimacy with your audience overriding the idea that we were watching distant critics. Instead you crafted a show where we felt we were observing very smart articulate friends, whose opinions mattered.

My sister Lisa bought me a David Stratton film course for my 22nd birthday. I still had not made a short film. The attendees were mostly retirees; in the break there was coffee in styrofoam cups and Arnott's Assorted. Every week I would go and watch a foreign film (the standout was Michael Powell's *Peeping Tom*) and listen to David riff. I was still at uni.

The film reviewed on *The Movie Show* that ended up mattering most to me was *See the Sea* by Francois Ozon, a 50-minute first feature with a limited release that I would never have seen if Margaret had not said it was important. That film still inspires me today. What a gem.

Gillian Armstrong, AM

is an internationally renowned Australian film director. Her films have been nominated for Academy and Golden Globe awards, and received Australian Film Institute, Film Critics Circle of Australia and the British Academy awards. Her credits include *My Brilliant Career, Starstruck, Charlotte Gray* and the documentary *Love, Lust & Lies.*

[Photo: Nick Cubbin]

all is forgiven

Gillian Armstrong

How wonderful, that this year's Don Dunstan Award is to a duo. A duo that we think of as one: *DavidandMargaret MargaretandDavid*

So different. Yet so perfect together. A brand all their own.

Who would have thought a director like myself, who has been reviewed, judged and her films dissected (not always particularly positively), would support such an accolade to a film critic!

My David/Margaret memories go back thirty-five years or more. Longhaired David, Director of the Sydney Film Festival, was one of the first to say kind words about my early short films and therefore my talent, i.e. confirming that I actually had some. And it was *completely* life affirming to have my little films up there on the screen in the glorious State Theatre in David's festival.

Whereas Margaret, a smart and lively blonde writer with a captivating husky laugh (which echoed up and down the stairs and through the editing room doors at Spectrum Films) was someone who was heading somewhere. Way before SBS and *The Movie Show*, our Margaret was always charging in and out of then husband Hans Pomeranz's postproduction house. It was there that she would have seen and developed her compassion and understanding of the ups and the bloody big downs and difficulties of the life of Aussie filmmakers. Yes, endless hours of passion and devotion creating that little film for it to be cut dead by one bad review. Spectrum was and is an institution, welcoming, supportive and generous to so many early Australian filmmakers. We were all there behind cutting-room doors or released into the light at the regular courtyard barbies.

And now Margaret, of that still very captivating laugh, is an *icon*.

David, fellow icon, with an obsessive love of films and film stars when a preschooler (a sure sign of an escapist and dreamer), had channelled his obsession into serious film appreciation and become key as a festival director and reviewer, assisting that new Australian filmmaking wave to be seen, screened and appreciated – uncensored!

Two such different personalities in taste, dress and humour but, importantly for the Australian industry and lovers of cinema, once brought together by Margaret at SBS they discovered they shared a passion. A passion for the art of cinema; for stories and actors (even if you did so often disagree over who was brilliant or endearing or just hopeless). It was their honesty, commitment and heartfelt dynamic that worked so well for us all.

It is important to have serious discussions that actually understand the craft of the director. They shared a real appreciation of the vision behind the camera angles, the lighting, editing, music and the casting. But most importantly, their reviewing was about the very heart of those films, the content and ethics.

Together they formed a lively, fiery, passionate, laughter-filled partnership. Yes, David, you fired up too when Ms Pomeranz stirred you into complete exasperation! The conflict worked, making the reviews more alive and insightful. It became a warm and entertaining, often hilarious, balancing act. And it connected with us all, whether filmmakers or mums and dads at home. I remember family dinners where each began to discuss what Margaret and David had said that week. All on first name terms, yet we had never met them. But they had entered our lives and living rooms and made us all film critics too!

They drew us into the debate. Yes we tried to hide the frustration and pain that David did not really get *Starstruck*, or that he hated Ralph Fiennes. And that Margaret really seemed to only like my documentaries. I think I've shouted at David once, or maybe twice, over the years. (And I don't think I was ever invited back to an SBS Christmas party.) And I could see it in their body language on camera, when they reviewed one of my films they don't love, even if there is an attempt to be luke-warm kind.

But you know what? Critics have no choice and we all admire them for it, their integrity. They are not swayed by friendships, or past history; they might have even completely misjudged and got it totally, totally wrong (please, David, have another look at *Oscar and Lucinda*) but that's their right and it's what we expect of a true critic.

I always looked forward to doing a David or Margaret interview. After a day of dealing with the same bland questions, it was a relief and delight to have a real film discussion; discussions that always drifted to Australian films and the need for more support for films.

Internationally, you could also see the filmmakers perk

up. Here were two people who loved and lived cinema, who engaged you with thoughtful and challenging questions.

Oh, we the audiences miss you and your insights and disagreements. And the art house cinemas and distributors certainly miss your sway! Thank you from the filmmakers and the industry and the festivals for your hard bloody work and integrity and compassion for stories and talent and cinema. For the fights against censorship and support for small local festivals and obscure, brave films. You should be proud of your incredibly powerful effect on generations of filmgoers, filmmakers and Australian culture in general.

And thank you from me. All is forgiven. Almost.

Andrew Mackie

is joint managing director of Transmission, a Sydney-based independent film distribution company. Its distributed films include *The King's Speech*, *Lion*, *Shame*, *Samson & Delilah*, *Calvary*, *Carol*, *Brooklyn* and *The Railway Man*.

something deeper

Andrew Mackie

When we heard Margaret and David were retiring, my business partner Richard Payten and I were devastated. Like everybody else we loved them. Of course, who doesn't? But for us there was another reason to worry, because while they themselves may not know it, Margaret and David's contribution to the business of Australian distribution and exhibition was considerable. Their on-screen retirement marked not just the end of a beloved weekly film-review show, but *something deeper*. To our antennae – the same ones we use to (rightly or wrongly) buy indie films to release in Australia via our company Transmission – it foretold the onset of a broader crisis.

The rise of high-quality television, a never-ending vomit

of free digital social content and the likes of DTV platforms like Netflix have redefined the economic boundaries of our business. The realm of cinema-as-church and primary water-cooler discussion topic are being relinquished. And as two of our cinemas most loved and vocal advocates stepped down, we knew that the old order of things was leaving forever and that film seemingly no longer commanded the mantel of Primary Art Form.

That was 2014, and things haven't been the same since. And *no* we aren't coping.

Disclaimer: chat to a film distributor long enough and sooner or later we'll complain about *something* ('bloody reviews', 'digital disruption', 'DVDs dying', 'sunny weather'). Only this time we aren't exaggerating. Margaret and David no longer having a weekly review show on Australian television? It only changed a fundamental mechanism in the way the independent end of the business operated.

It's mostly about cut-through. With between five-to-ten films released each week, how do smaller independent movies make their existence known? And as print media declines, with the arts staff usually among the first to walk the plank, film critics with substantial audience reach are becoming an endangered species.

And you're seeing the impact unfold on cinema screens:

'comfort films' reign. There's nobody with the power of Margaret and David's audience saying 'take a chance on this weird-looking Italian film', or 'trust us and see *A Separation*'. The audience is moving as a pack in a seemingly uninformed manner, left to their own devices, rewarding average 'arthouse' movies wrapped in marketing campaigns that promise non-confrontational vanilla experiences over challenging, rewarding true arthouse films designed to provoke or defy the formula. True arthouse movies are increasingly ignored, regardless of accolades received in Cannes, Venice, Sundance or Berlin.

The gears of distribution have reacted accordingly, no longer relying on or susceptible to the power of reviews to reassure audiences that this movie is worth your time. In an era where everybody is a reviewer, and reviews are aggregated to a score, the joy of engagement and discovery is waning in the face of abundance. And even though we hated it when Margaret or David rated one of our releases poorly, we took it on the chin. But when we scored big ('**** – Margaret and David!') we'd build entire advertisements around that score. Transmission was thrice blessed with the holy grail: the mythical ten-star review (*Good Night, and Good Luck*, *Amour*, *Samson & Delilah*, which were incidentally all arthouse hits that proportionally over-performed here in Australia). We estimated a double-five-star score was worth $300,000 additional box office, minimum. Compare this to a small film winning a Best Film Oscar, which can add at least $500,000 to $1 million to its tally (*Moonlight*, for example, was pulling up stumps at around $1.5 million before its Best Picture win took it on to a $2.5 million final result). Even a double four-star score was something to sing from the rooftops, often boosting box office by $200,000 to $300,000.

Even when they disagreed, the joy of conflict meant it wasn't the end of the world in terms of putting bums on seats. In fact, it was one of the pros when we were evaluating whether to buy Lars von Trier's *Antichrist* (David was certain to dislike it, but the entertainment value of their fireworks guaranteed a level of audience curiosity and attention).

Now, in 2017 PMD (post Margaret & David), thematically or visually challenging foreign-language films and edgier auteur cinema are increasingly limited to film festival exposure rather than general release. And despite a handful of experienced film critics still working in the medium there remains a growing void where Margaret and David once sat. Their show was the campfire that triggered discourse and debate, drawing attention to the films that didn't have expensive advertising campaigns to make their presence felt.

So in their public absence it is up to all of us now. We are all Margaret and David. Go to a film festival. Take a risky chance at the cinema. But most of all, argue about movies with your friends. *At the Movies* is gone, so it is up to those who value the diversity of cinema to step into their shoes.

Thank you, David, Australia's cinema dad, the erudite shaggy-faced bellwether of film opinion. Thank you, Margaret, for your passion, insight and sexy gravel-voiced tones. As exhibitors and distributors, we can't thank you both enough for loving cinema, spreading all those stars around, and continuing to be so active behind the scenes as supporters and advocates for the culture of film. We have two seats at the ready anytime you decide to change your minds.

Sandra Levy, AO

director, producer and board member, has played a pivotal
role in film and television in Australia in the last thirty years.
She has held senior positions at ABC TV (including Director
of Television) and Channel 9, and at independent production
companies Southern Star and Zapruder's Other Films.
She was appointed CEO of the Australian Film, Television and
Radio School in 2007 and served nine years.

bear witness

Sandra Levy

t's 1997 and we are at the Cannes Film Festival. We are walking up the red carpeted stairs of the Palais, while the theme music of our film is broadcast to the paparazzi and crowds lined up at the front of the building.

We are the official group. Director, actors, distributors, financiers. We had arrived in designated cars with the Cannes Festival flag flying up front and now, on cue, we walk slowly up the steps to be welcomed by the head of the Festival. We shake hands, smile and then on instruction turn to face the paparazzi. As our music fills the air and the paps snaps photos of our beautiful cast and director, I look out across the Croisette, across the heads of the crowds, and am startled by the sudden rush of tears and emotion.

There is the Australian flag, tied to the SBS office balcony, on a building opposite the Palais. And there are Margaret and David, waving to us. Maybe I imagine them there. I probably can't see them. But I feel they are there sharing this moment of great pride with us, as we represent our country. This little film at the film Olympics. And the two people who know and love the film industry and understand the importance of this festival and our selection are there to witness it. As they have been for so many other Australian filmmakers. And will be for so many more in the future.

We all watched *The Movie Show* on SBS to learn more about film – hear the reviews, interviews, discussions, learn about festivals, share the love of film. We loved the wonderful contrast in character, the scholarly David, the impetuous and passionate Margaret, took pleasure in the endless discourse, the endless differences of opinion and approach. How we loved it.

When I was Head of Television at the ABC I naturally wanted a film show for the ABC audience just as good as *The Movie Show*. We talked about who else could be hosts of a film show. We might even have tried some out. Always the model was Margaret and David. To find someone just like them, as good as them, as exciting to watch, who really loved film, and knew a lot about it. Experts but not dull and academic – but perhaps just a little academic, like David, with someone lively and lovely like Margaret.

And then I was at an event one night and Margaret was there. We were talking about what had been happening at SBS. David's film introductions had been dropped. There was a mood for change there and it seemed as if they were not being treated well. Spontaneously I said come to us, to the ABC. It was a perfect idea. I should have thought of it before! Margaret was surprised, maybe even shocked. Always loyal to SBS she wanted to think about it, and to talk to David.

She loved SBS, and was apprehensive about the ABC. There was a lot of discussion between them. It wasn't an easy decision and took considerable time but finally they both decided to do it.

And then began twelve months of secret negotiations, secret commissioning and contracts and planning and set designs and ideas for the best time slot. It was important that Margaret and David chose the right time to tell SBS and their audience and the film industry what they were about to do. I had to ensure the information didn't leak out, it felt a real test of the organisation they were nervously joining. Could we keep their secret and respect their decision?

We did, and they did. Come to the ABC. Very successfully and for a long time. And their audience for *At the Movies* grew in size and affection over the years, and everyone in the country now knows them by their first names. Comedy sketches affectionately send them up, for their foibles and idiosyncrasies, and for just being Margaret and David.

Their on-screen skirmishes of the mind are legend. They are rightly loved and admired for many things, for above all being themselves, being true to who they are, to their values, to their judgements, to their deep and knowledgeable love of film. All of us in the film industry feel connected to them, our films have been reviewed by them, we have seen them at our key events, we have become friends with them and shared their love of film. We have passionately agreed or passionately disagreed with their opinions over the years. They have mattered to each and every one of us who love film.

Nashen Moodley

is the Director of the Sydney Film Festival. During his
six years at the helm, the Festival has grown significantly.
Moodley's career in film programming has encompassed
leadership roles as Manager and Head of Programming at the
Durban International Film Festival (2001–2011)
and as a programming consultant for the
Dubai International Film Festival (2005–present).

love letter

Nashen Moodley

This is a love letter to Margaret and David: to their love of cinema, to their unending determination to ensure that cinema culture thrives, and to their championing of films that really need champions.

I arrived in Australia to take on the role of Sydney Film Festival Director, sadly only in time to catch the final years of the seminal *At the Movies*, but the impact was clear to see. Margaret Pomeranz and David Stratton with their intelligent, knowing and entertaining film reviews had a vast influence on moviegoers; a positive review could really bring a big audience to a film. Their knowledgeable reviews could make seemingly challenging cinema accessible to a broader audience. I saw that firsthand during my first festival. A very positive review of Nuri Bilge Ceylan's *Once Upon a Time in Anatolia* led to the film selling more than 2000 tickets at a single screening at the Sydney Film Festival. It's a great film, no doubt, but at close to three hours not an obvious big seller. It's but one example I can venture of their incredible influence in bringing unusual cinema to broader attention.

I met David first, soon after arriving in Sydney. He had famously held the role of Sydney Film Festival Director for eighteen remarkable years. In this first meeting David told me about his time as the director, his battles with censorship, his wonderful experiences travelling the world and negotiating on films directly with their makers. We also spoke about African cinema and David expressed a desire to visit South Africa – a place he'd never been. I encouraged him to do so at some point, ideally at a time when I was there so we could spend some time together.

Much to my surprise, a few weeks later I heard from David that he had booked his trip to South Africa and looked forward to seeing me there. We did meet there and I took David and his wife Susie to my favourite restaurant in Durban. He started the meal by asking me to name my favourite film. The answer passed muster, I trust, and we proceeded to an enjoyable dinner.

Later I met Margaret, and was moved by her kindness and willingness to help. A person of broad interests, we've had Margaret spend a night on stage at the festival, just after spending hours at a street protest against the treatment of refugees. Earlier this year, she served as President of the Jury for the Official Competition and it was wonderful to see her presiding over a diverse group of people with divergent opinions; gently guiding them to a decision while allowing each of them to freely express their opinions.

Since I've met David and Margaret, I've asked much of them. Each year I've worked on the Sydney Film Festival, Margaret and David have made a significant contribution – David hosting several talks and programming significant retrospectives, and Margaret chairing panels, conducting onstage interviews and Q&As, hosting award ceremonies, and serving as President of the Jury. In 2015, the festival hosted an event at the Sydney Town Hall in which the two regaled the vast audience with the topic: The Films We Love: The Neglected and the Unexpected. Never have they declined a request, and I owe each of them more favours than I can count. I am not the only one. They maintain a significant presence at many Australian and international film festivals and events.

One of the joys of knowing them, of course, is talking

about films. An observation: it seems to me that David is firm in his opinion immediately after the film ends, while Margaret takes more time to reflect. These different approaches, each with advantages, have perhaps played a part in their successful and endearing collaboration.

This is a love letter to Margaret and David. Their contribution to film culture in this country is monumental; and it seems likely that we'll never see the likes of them again. Thank you, dear Margaret and David, for all you have done, continue to do, and will do for a long time to come.

Josh Pomeranz

is managing director of Spectrum Films, Australia's leading post-production house based in Fox Studios Australia. Recent productions include *Alien: Covenant*, *Lion*, *Gods of Egypt* and *The Great Gatsby*. Josh's management has continued to foster the company's stellar reputation as the post-production facility of choice for feature films, television productions and documentaries.

how wrong we were

Josh Pomeranz

I was a pre-teen when Mum started on *The Movie Show*. It was the 1980s and I still remember the family meeting in our sunroom to discuss it while I daydreamed about playing cricket on the street. I had no comprehension of the journey it would take us on. None of us did. Nor did I have the maturity to recognise that this would be a defining moment for our family, or the amazing journey ahead.

Our family is small. In that sunroom was my brother Felix, who is now working in VFX on *Star Wars*, my late father Hans Pomeranz, who founded Spectrum Films in 1964, and myself, now running Spectrum. Mum, was just Mum. She helped us with our homework, cooked dinners (her cooking is so much better now) and navigated the northern beaches of Sydney so we could play soccer on Saturday mornings, often stressing about the opening times of the Spit Bridge. These were the salad days.

Without many reservations, we all decided to support Mum in this new, unknown role. 'It'll be cool, Mum, if you really want to be on TV. It's only SBS. No one will watch anyway, except my French and German teachers at school.' How wrong we were.

Her partnership with David Stratton would be one of the longest in Australian TV and my family watched in awe (and surprise) as they and the show gained more and more recognition; as Margaret and David and their little show crept into the Australian consciousness. They would become a staple within Australian TV and film culture, though Mum couldn't understand what all the fuss was about.

Our mum was now a professional presenter and producer. And she was good at it. I had the most respect for the way she produced and I wished she had done more of it. She led by example. She was fiercely loyal, hardworking and lots of fun. She had the most supportive of teams over many years. She worked hard and fought for a financially challenged public broadcaster, which she is so passionate about. She still gets together with members of the team. The respect is mutual.

Suddenly our family had grown. She and David have been encouraging their audience to see films for more than thirty years and have passionately championed Australian movies. She has always been in love with the arts in this country.

She left Australia in her twenties to enrich her life, complaining about the banality of Sydney at the time. Her escapism was cinema. She wanted to teach us the power of film and the influence it has on a nation's culture. It is essential nourishment, as she often tells me. She loves a multicultural Australia. Having married a Jewish Dutch immigrant, I have seen firsthand the contribution my father has made to this country.

When I was eight, Mum and her best friend Robyn Sinclair took me, Felix and Robyn's daughter Helen through India and up into Kashmir to Srinagar, where we trekked through the Himalayas. Two single mums on an adventure, trying to show their kids a different world to the priviliged one we were used to. I almost lost my life up there on horseback, only to be saved by the tiny Kashmiri cook who was travelling with us. Mum was shaken, but secretly buzzed with the thought we were all out of our comfort zones. I don't know if Dad ever knew how close it was.

Margaret's biggest problem is saying no. She tirelessly

champions anything that has to do with the silver screen, the arts in this country, public broadcasting, censorship. She stoically defends the rights of adults to have a choice, being a former president on Watch on Censorship. I was there at the Town Hall in Balmain when she was escorted offstage by police after 'illegally' screening Ken Park, controversially banned after failing to receive classification from the Office of Film and Literature. It was packed to the rafters. Everyone roared when she ran back to push play on the DVD player. She has always lived by her credo of standing up for what you believe in. To this day, her diary is full, taking on duties she feels obliged and mostly honoured to do because of her position.

The thing I most admire about Mum is her work ethic. She never does anything halfheartedly. She'll work all hours to deliver on time and hates being unprofessional. She takes huge pride in her work, whether it's working for SBS, the ABC or, now, Foxtel, writing for the *Medical Observer*, or running around Cannes. People say to me, 'Oh what fun for your mum – the south of France.' I have seen it firsthand, it is no holiday. She runs herself ragged, fuelled by adrenaline and the adage, a deadline is a deadline. She will work until the chorus of dawn embraces another day in order to deliver.

She is a fantastic listener. She'll stop and talk to anyone who engages, often to our frustration. And she has total respect for her position, and has never taken it for granted. How blessed her life has been, she tells me.

I remember *The Movie Show* parties at our house with Peter Weir, Rosanna Arquette, Philip Noyce, Gillian Armstrong and an endless list of talent holding court. Everyone was welcome; Mum was a great entertainer, making everyone feel at home. And the parties were well known. I probably took it for granted.

She cherished her times at SBS and the ABC. She hated leaving SBS, it did not sit well with her. It was not an easy decision but it was made on principle, a vote against the direction the network was heading. She loved the ABC – the big time as far as public broadcasting goes. Bigger exposure, more responsibility. She revelled in it. Though she gave up producing the show. It was sad when David and Margaret's time came to an end. There were Cate Blanchett and Geoffrey Rush playing their alter egos in the lead-up to their final show together.

Finally, the biggest question people still ask me about Margaret and David is whether they get on. 'They fight all the time on screen, surely they must dislike each other.' It surprises me. How could two people who have worked together so closely over thirty years not be friends?

For me it's obvious, David is one of Mum's dearest friends and the foundation of this pairing has been their unconditional friendship and care for each other. They refer to each other as Moj and Stratts. Best friends forever, and dedicated film critics.

Felix and I are incredibly proud of you, Mum. The mother on TV with the funny earrings, reviewing movies for a living. Who would have thought?

Geoffrey Rush, AC

is an actor with an incredible list of plays and films to his credit. He won international recognition and acclaim, and numerous awards including an Oscar, Golden Globe, British Film Award and Australian Film Institute Award for his portrayal of David Helfgott in *Shine*. His other films include *Shakespeare in Love*, *The Eye of the Storm*, *The King's Speech* and the *Pirates of the Caribbean* series.

a toast

Geoffrey Rush

Geoffrey Rush toasts Margaret and David as they leave our screens following the final episode of ABC TV's At the Movies, *December 2014.*

As Shakespeare lamented when he chronicled a royal departure:

Hung be the heavens with black, yield day to night.
Comets importing change of times and states,
Brandish your crystal tresses in the sky ...

As we say goodbye to *At the Movies*, there is a sadness in the air. Not the sort of sadness, say, like when Michael Corleone had Fredo shot in a fishing boat saying his Hail Mary's (*Godfather* Part 2 1974) ...

Or sad the way Dirk Bogarde's make-up ran down his temples on a beach (*Death in Venice* 1971) ...

Or even sad the way Bambi had to flee a forest fire and was separated from his doe-eyed girlfriend Falina (Disney-RKO release 1942) ...

Or even *really* sad in an *Old Yeller*/*Marley and Me*/*Red Dog* kind of way – or an unavoidable *My Left Foot*-ish/*Imitation of Life*-like/*ET*-esque/*Fault is in the Stars*/*The Notebook*-y syndrome.

Perhaps it's more curiously melancholic like Charlie Chaplin and Paulette Goddard finally walking down the road together to the strains of 'Smile' (*Modern Times* 1936), or Adele Exarchopoulos walking down yet another street in her life to a brave but unknown future at the end of *Blue Is The Warmest Colour* (2013).

No. It is because the Australian film industry is a little bit poorer at losing 'Margaret and David' from our TV screens – and that means we're losing part of our filmmaking family.

When Cate Blanchett and I playfully reviewed your 25th anniversary we critiqued you as an epic romantic comedy about a film critic couple who live together in an Australian television studio. We quipped that the concept of two people talking in armchairs for so many years could have been tedious beyond belief.

It wasn't. Ever.

We cited you as a unique couple, comparable to Laurel and Hardy, Hepburn and Tracy – or even *Alien* vs *Predator*. For twenty-eight years your sparkling bickering has been entertaining and enlightening. Every week you dished up the grit, the grammar, the poetry from the international and local, the contemporary and heritage catalogue. Your yin and yang opinions presented neat snapshots of an uncompromised smorgasbord from blockbusters to indies. We dreamed you would eternally be sitting in those chairs.

All of us here tonight have drunkenly argued and brawled at dinner parties, emulating your snazzy badinage, but we were always in awe that you could do that week after week for close to three decades – sober!

Thank you, David, for your scholarly elegance and for appointing the irreplaceable Margaret and enthroning her on your right – our screen left, the place where the Western eye naturally gravitates. Maybe selfishly you thought the show might have been franchised to Al Jazeera TV and the focus was to be on you.

It was on you both.

And thank you, Margaret, for being an instinctive, informed, intelligent woman rightfully claiming your full-blooded fifty per cent of our national screen. So treasured – and too rare.

You would readily reference *Amarcord* ('I remember'), Fellini's autobiographical fantasia from 1973 – your musical theme for the SBS years came from this film: Nino Rota's '*Il Manine di Primavera*', The Enfolding Arms of Spring. On this warm early December night, this music couldn't be more poignant as we bid you farewell. But you in fact chose its rowdier circus incarnation from Fellini's earlier 1971 documentary *The Clowns* – a Maguffin that told us you took your work seriously but, most endearingly, not yourselves.

In your migration to the ABC you threw down a symbolic gauntlet as you chose Supersonic composers Paul Healy and Antony Partos (both BA graduates in Sound from our Film and Television school) to write theme music as potent as the ABC news fanfare and funkier than our national anthem.

I remember your very first episode on *The Movie Show*: you reviewed and supported *The Fringe-Dwellers*. On your debut program for *At the Movies* it was *Touching the Void*. May neither fringe-dwelling nor void-touching define either of your future journeys.

I doubt you will ever be surpassed. We understand and respect your decision. We shall try to comprehend the new world order of 'efficiency dividends' – (whatever the fuck that means).

Let this be neither a wake nor a roast; I'm here to propose a most thankful toast.

Composer Casey Bennetto captured it perfectly in his lyric:

> *I turn myself around*
> *I pull myself apart*
> *There's a David in my head*
> *And a Margaret in my heart.*

On behalf of our industry I want to thank you for these twenty-eight years. My numerological friends tell me certain numbers are considered sacred and magical: seven and its multiples are symbols of perfection, effectiveness and completeness.

We all want to applaud you, because every culture needs its champions – and tonight, Margaret and David, you are most certainly ours.

Adolfo Aranjuez

is editor of *Metro*, Australia's oldest film and media periodical.
He is also subeditor of *Screen Education* and a freelance writer,
speaker and dancer. He has edited for *Liminal*, *Voiceworks*
and Melbourne Books, and been published in *Right Now*,
The Lifted Brow, *Overland*, *The Manila Review*,
Eureka Street and *Peril*, among others.

critical opinion is critical

Adolfo Aranjuez

There's a gustatory quality to our responses to art – we love to *eat up* what's *tasteful*; we're repelled by what's *gross*; it can be *stomach-churning* or *tough to swallow*. It's no surprise, then, that these reactions are often driven by instinct: like food, art's impact is felt in the gut. What makes cinema even more affecting is its high level of verisimilitude: we feel as though we're transported to a milieu that reflects – or perhaps reveals possibilities for – our own, and this mimetic quality cajoles us into projecting the values we hold in the real world onto its representational counterpart.

But one of my biggest takeaways from Margaret Pomeranz and David Stratton's prolific output is to always temper gut-based judgments with critical ones. Their job may have required them to confer a numerical rating on each film they reviewed – a reductive critical system if there ever was one – but their opinions never ended there. Rather than just voicing the ways in which a film, say, *leaves a bad taste in the mouth*, they contextualised each work, historicised it, made reference to the canon, challenged us to weigh up its shortcomings against its successes. Through example, they taught me – both as someone who writes criticism and as an editor responsible for commissioning the work of others – that a good critic ensures each piece of commentary is bolstered with erudition and evidence. A good critic doesn't just intuit displeasure, but interrogates why a particular scene generates discomfort, or why a certain character is so unlikeable, or why a filmmaker might have opted for one stylistic flourish over another.

Beyond going with our gut, we also tend to measure the worth of art against its moral weightiness. The relationship between aesthetics and ethics is certainly complicated, but it's understandable as well, given both are exercises in evaluation. As novelist–philosopher Iris Murdoch has written, engaging with art entails 'unselfing' – it affords us opportunities to make sense of life through different eyes. When we watch a film about murder, we're compelled to inquire about motive; when we see violence, we're forced to ask about the viability of choice and the very real constraints of circumstance.

When, in 1992, Geoffrey Wright's *Romper Stomper* polarised Margaret and David (the former deemed it brutal yet brave, while the latter dismissed it as irresponsible), what the pair essentially butted heads about was the film's apparent *moral* objectives: in depicting race-based skirmishes with vividness and vigour, though without overt condemnation, was Wright censuring the violence on show or sympathising with it? The disagreement has become infamous in Australian cinema history, not least because it is a rare case of a critic refusing to rate a film outright. Nevertheless, it does highlight the centrality of informed critical opinion: David's reproach rested on legitimate fears about life imitating art, *Romper Stomper* plausibly inflaming real-world racial tensions.

Here, we see a significant aspect of the critic's role: that of cultural arbiter. I don't mean this in the sense that critics are 'special', occupying a pedestal above the average viewer – though, of course, critics possess special*ist* knowledge that they must wield in order to level educated critique. Nor am I celebrating the critic as gatekeeper – while I agreed with Margaret's plea in a 2014 op-ed that local films could benefit from 'a bit of kindness', it has been demonstrated, time and again, that the correlation between positive reviews and positive box-office performance is shaky at best. Rather, I'm alluding to how critics must mediate between creator and consumer. In the words of famed critic Roger Ebert, the act of criticism is a 'balancing act' between popular engagement and more highbrow examination.

This is possibly a contentious assertion on my part, but I don't believe artists are obligated to make their message plain for their audience. This isn't to say that great art shouldn't have affect – quite the contrary, as, for me, that is the most powerful thing. Sometimes, however, the beauty of an artwork lies in non-literality, in enigma; and sometimes, artists don't themselves have a complete grasp on what they're trying to convey, emotional impact notwithstanding. It falls to the critic, therefore, to translate the work for the audience, to navigate the codes and conventions underpinning it; identify the influences nodded to; unpack what's in the frame using the frameworks of history, finance and contemporary sociopolitics.

In a way, then, the critic embodies the quintessential representative of the culture – appreciative; astute; willing to approach an artwork, be affronted, and then articulate the whys and wherewithals of arriving at such an opinion.

They can be an advocate of individual creations or even the broader industry, as Margaret has championed, or an adversary, as per David's grievances against *Romper Stomper*. Ultimately, though, it's the conversations that critics inspire that count the most – even when sending a dish back to the kitchen, we need to be able to say exactly what about it we find distasteful and why.

Al Clark

has produced films for the past thirty-two years, first in the
UK – where his credits include *Nineteen Eighty-Four, Absolute
Beginners* and *Gothic* – then in Australia. His Australian
films – which have been selected for most major film festivals
and distributed worldwide – include *The Adventures of Priscilla,
Queen of the Desert, Chopper, Blessed* and the forthcoming
Flammable Children. The recipient of the 2013 AACTA
Raymond Longford Award for lifetime achievement, and
appointed to the board of Screen Australia in December 2014,
he is also the author of two books,
Raymond Chandler in Hollywood and *Making Priscilla*.

cannes 1997

Al Clark

No matter how well one knows people, or for how long, sometimes it's a single moment that defines them in the memory.

Cannes 1997. There's a party in full swing in a palatial function room at the Hotel Majestic, the only luxury hotel directly across the road from the Palais des Festivals itself – although celebrities routinely take a limo from here to the beginning of the red carpet a hundred metres away.

Under the chandeliers, Margaret is in full swing too, as convivial and companionable a presence as one could hope to encounter in such a setting, where the shrill simulation of unerring self-confidence is practically deafening.

David, looking a little anxious, interrupts our conversation. He tells Margaret that she must join him outside urgently to make a presentation to camera in front of the Palais, where the crew awaits them.

Margaret is reluctant to leave, and resists accordingly.

'I can't,' she declares, 'I'm talking to Al.'

David, standing right next to me, says, 'Fuck Al,' and drags her off.

Richard Kuipers

is a film critic for the international trade paper *Variety* and a
documentary film producer. His credits include *Stone Forever*
and *The Cambodian Space Project – Not Easy Rock'n'Roll*.
Richard produced *The Movie Show*
from 1992 to 2000.

part of the family

Richard Kuipers

t's the middle of 1996. I've been producing *The Movie Show* at SBS since 1992. In a few months the show will be ten years old. I'm just about to start digging through the archives to prepare a tenth anniversary special. But Margaret and David have something bigger on their minds. They've decided that a decade is a great run and it's time to quit while they're still on top. In December 1996 *The Movie Show* will finish. Well, that was the plan ...

As the end of the year drew closer and after the birthday edition had been broadcast the conversation changed to: 'Oh, let's just give it one more year.' Thankfully for viewers and the Australian film industry 'one more year' became eighteen.

When *The Movie Show* turned fifteen in 2001, the *Sydney Morning Herald* asked Margaret and David about the show's longevity. As always, they told it straight.

'I wouldn't have foreseen fifteen minutes,' said David. Margaret elaborated: 'We started something on SBS with no one watching, so we were able to be really horrible on air for a long period without too many people noticing.' It's well known today that *The Movie Show* went to air in 1986 without anyone in senior management actually having seen it. This is a perfect example of what made SBS the best and most exciting broadcaster in the universe at that time. Where else in the world of public television could that possibly have happened? What's less well known is how unpolished and downright clunky *The Movie Show* was in its infancy. As I plucked dusty old tapes from the shelves in 1996 and watched those early episodes it struck me that if *The Movie Show* had been made anywhere else but SBS it would have been lucky to last one season. But this was SBS in the 1980s, when experiments were encouraged, new talent from diverse backgrounds was being discovered, management looked favourably on staff that had constructive criticism to offer, and huge risks were part of the unspoken charter. Most importantly, new programs such as *The Movie Show* were given the chance to improve and grow up in public.

SBS bosses might not have looked too closely at the start but they were smart enough to see what the whole country would soon know: David Stratton and Margaret Pomeranz had genuine screen chemistry and each possessed sincerity that couldn't be bought or taught. All they needed was time to get into the groove. Plenty of time, but what a superb investment it turned out to be. As with just about everyone that ever worked on *The Movie Show* I was a film fanatic and a huge fan of the show who could barely believe my good fortune when I started working with Margaret and David. I'd been at SBS since 1988 as camera operator, production assistant and floor manager. As floor manager you see and hear everything. What I witnessed in the late '80s and early '90s during *The Movie Show* recordings was the slow and superb evolution of Margaret and David and the show itself. Gone was the draggy pace and stiffness that dogged those early days. In its place was the spark and sizzle that made David and Margaret an unbeatable screen team.

By 1992 and the famous *Romper Stomper* discussion they'd well and truly hit their stride. It was one of their finest moments – but not for the reasons usually associated with it, such as the film's writer–director Geoffrey Wright hurling that glass of wine at David. Usually we allocated forty-five seconds or a minute at most for discussions. This one ran for nearly three minutes. Four-and-a-half stars from Margaret. No score from David. Not zero, but firmly detailed reasons as to why he felt he could not score the film. There'd never been a discussion quite like this before, and there never would be again. It was electrifying to watch in the studio and made for amazing television. What made it really extraordinary to me was the manner in which David and Margaret conducted themselves before, during and after that discussion. As far apart as they'd ever been on a film – and an Australian film, no less – both argued their cases superbly. For viewers, here was the supreme moment of Margaret and David being equal but different.

Working with Margaret and David for nine years was, to put it simply, a dream. The energy, enthusiasm, absolute love of cinema and passionate support for the Australian film industry that Margaret and David delivered every Wednesday night reflected the atmosphere inside the show's production team. When we worked on *The Movie Show* we were more than just a producer, director, production manager or production assistant. We were part of a family. Everyone had creative input into the show. The weekly thirty-second promo was edited by the production assistant. Production managers weren't stuck in the office doing paperwork the whole time. We'd go out on shoots when stars were interviewed or we did a set report from the dozens of Australian films visited. If we had a good idea for a story, we went ahead and shot it. When a production assistant called one morning and said she was too distraught to come to work because Ginger Rogers had just died I understood completely. It was that sort of workplace. Everyone did a part of everyone else's job and everyone belonged to a tight-knit family that had one goal only – to make the best possible half-hour of television we could, forty-four times a year on average.

We did things differently. When those dreadful (and now thoroughly discredited) workstations were installed at SBS we refused to have them. We'll keep our desks and the proper lines of communication they afford, thank you. As the '90s rolled on and ghastly corporate initiatives such as 'key performance indicators' and 'performance appraisal reviews' crept into SBS, Margaret smelled a big and insidious rat. These work practices were clearly devised to increase the power of upper management by destroying team morale and turning co-workers against each other. We took matters into our own hands and treated these reports with the contempt they deserved. Margaret was so much more than a fabulous film critic. She was our inspirational executive producer who could spot bullshit a mile away and prevent it from getting anywhere near *The Movie Show*.

While Margaret wrangled things brilliantly on the home front, David gave *The Movie Show* team the best film education we could ever hope for. Apart from the incredible knowledge and immaculately droll sense of humour he brought to the mix David would often invite us to all-day movie marathons at his home (and a special thanks here to the wonderful Susie Stratton). We called it our Big Day Out. From his astonishing collection of VHS tapes, laserdiscs (!) and those new-fangled DVDs David would select four and sometimes five gems no one had seen before (not an easy task, but he never failed). Complete with fully fledged introductions and post-screening discussions that would go anywhere and everywhere, David opened our eyes to dozens of fantastic films such as *Never Let Go* (1960), *Midnight* (1939), *Green For Danger* (1946), *The Green Man* (1956), *A Lawless Street* (1955), and any number of hard-boiled crime pics in which tough guys like Jack Palance, Richard Widmark and Lee Marvin slapped a lot of other guys around.

In these big and small ways David and Margaret created a rare and very special environment at *The Movie Show* and it showed in the program we made together. It was the most natural thing in the world for everyone, including David and Margaret, to go above and beyond the call of duty. Just as Margaret and David had no interest in being celebrities themselves, the show had no interest in celebrity gossip and other trivial matters. It was always about the films and nothing else.

David and Margaret's personal integrity established *The Movie Show*'s reputation in Australia and brought amazing rewards when we travelled. Even though our weekly audience was only a fraction of most other television shows competing for interviews at these international film festivals *The Movie Show* was usually placed at the head of the queue. When Roman Polanski only gave three television interviews in Cannes, we got one. When the great American filmmaker Robert Altman granted an extremely rare, career-spanning interview in Cannes it was because Margaret Pomeranz had requested it. Kenneth Branagh and Emma Thompson invited *The Movie Show* to Tuscany while they were having a jolly good time making *Much Ado About Nothing*. And let's not forget the first-ever television interview of Quentin Tarantino. That honour goes to David Stratton in Cannes, 1992, just before *Reservoir Dogs* caught fire. I'll never forget it. David's first question was 'What are some of your influences?' Twenty-four minutes later

Quentin stopped talking. Then he asked us to send him a tape of the interview because he'd never been on TV before! Solid gold. When David interviewed Nikita Mikhalkov for *Burnt by the Sun* in 1994, the Russian master leapt up and gave David a giant bear hug. The hilarious American actor Seymour Cassel even planted a couple of kisses on David (while cameras were still rolling) after they'd talked about *In the Soup* (1992).

How did this television show with such a small audience become such a respected and important part of the international film scene? Margaret and David's skill and stature, that's how. As *The Movie Show* continued to cover major festivals, 'David and Margaret from Australia' became known as outstanding interviewers who cared passionately about world cinema and never asked stupid questions about anyone's personal lives. Filmmakers and publicists knew that a positive reaction from *The Movie Show* could play a role in films securing an Australian distributor. When indie filmmakers such as Hal Hartley (*The Unbelievable Truth, Trust*) and Whit Stillman (*Metropolitan, Barcelona*) spoke to us in Cannes and Venice about their films 'doing well in Australia', at least part of the credit has to go to David and Margaret's critical support. There is no question that positive reviews from *The Movie Show* and *At the Movies* translated into significant box-office earnings for many art-house films and Australian productions. Since *At the Movies* finished in November 2014 I'm certain that Australian film distributors think twice about acquiring small and often risky films that in previous years would have at least stood a fighting chance with David and Margaret's seal of critical approval.

While smaller Australian distributors were eager to hold preview screenings the same wasn't always the case with larger companies handling Hollywood studio product. When dud films came along there would often be no press screening, and therefore no potentially negative *Movie Show* review on the Wednesday night before Thursday release. In the case of stinkers, it was annoying but understandable. But when Roadshow refused to preview *Interview with the Vampire* in 1994 we took exception. Here's one of the most anticipated films of the year, starring Brad Pitt and Tom Cruise and directed by Neil Jordan straight after his triumph with *The Crying Game*. As always, Margaret had a brilliant solution. It involved flying David to Hawaii, where the film had just opened, then flying him back to Sydney in just enough time to record the show. Hey, presto! The review goes to air (four stars as I remember) and Roadshow is left wondering how we pulled it off. I kept David's Hawaii admission ticket for proof, just in case.

Whenever SBS or anyone else tried to turn Margaret and David into 'stars' they'd have none of it. Margaret always said, 'There's no way I'm ever going to have my face on the side of a bus.' Of course they were stars whether they liked it or not. That's simply what happens when you're that good. But they never sought the limelight and never acted like stars. That's part of the reason they were so adored by television viewers, and remain so today. It's also a major reason why *The Movie Show* and *At the Movies* maintained such high standards for twenty-eight years. They were just as well loved by the production teams around them as the viewing public. This showed up on screen, week after week, year after year. While David and Margaret certainly had some ferocious off-screen arguments in those years it was always about a film (surprise!) or an issue related to the film industry. Something worth fighting about, and never personal.

Margaret and David are dear friends whose incredible generosity and support has helped me incalculably, both personally and professionally. I became a film critic after my stint on *The Movie Show* and whatever I know about that profession I most surely learned from them. So many people involved in the Australian film industry will have their own stories of when Margaret Pomeranz and David Stratton made a huge impact on their lives and careers.

Whether it's audiences who've lost two of the most loved and respected presenters in Australian television history or the many branches of the Australian film industry that looked to *The Movie Show* and *At the Movies* for recognition and support, David and Margaret's retirement has left a void that will most likely never be filled. Not bad for a television show that began in 1986 when SBS had a half-hour gap in the schedule and Margaret Pomeranz put her hand in the air and said, 'I've got an idea.'

Kath Shelper and Warwick Thornton's

working partnership began with the short film *Green Bush*,
which premiered at Sundance and won the Panorama Prize at
the Berlinale Film Festival, 2005. Their first feature, *Samson &
Delilah*, won the Camera d'Or prize at Cannes Film Festival in
2009 after first premiering at Adelaide Film Festival.

stars in our eyes

Kath Shelper and
Warwick Thornton

When we were budding young(ish) filmmakers, all we wanted to do was graduate to making feature films so we could be reviewed by Margaret and David. To hear them argue over the lead actor's performance or talk about the abuse of the handheld cinematography. For Margaret to screech, *David!* with that gorgeous throaty laugh of hers. And David to conclude that he 'found it a bit tedious to be perfectly honest'.

When it came our turn, we couldn't have written the script better. We heard that Margaret was attending an early private screening of *Samson & Delilah* in Sydney before our world premiere at the Adelaide Film Festival. We were shitting ourselves. This was the big test. This would mean we were heroes or we were zeroes. Or maybe just three stars. Not great, not terrible. Average.

We arrived at the Adelaide Film Festival to a schedule of media interviews that kicked off with Margaret interviewing Warwick for *At the Movies*. The interview was taking place in a small room above a shopfront in Rundle Street. Warwick disappeared up the stairs. The old floorboards squeaked as he moved into the room. And then all went silent. For, what felt like, an eternity. We waited below, nervous and pacing. After a while, Warwick emerged with a big grin on his face. Maybe even a tear in his eye. Well? She loves it. She fucking loves it. It was the most beautiful interview, I loved the conversation, I love her. I love everyone. But what is love? Is love three-and-a-half stars? May we dare to dream that love is four stars?

It was my turn to ascend the staircase and face Margaret. Amber Ma, the producer of the show, told me that she had goosebumps on her arms while she was listening to Warwick talk to Margaret. A hard act to follow, but I did my best and got my own special dose of Margaret charm.

David still hadn't seen the film – we knew he was going to watch it at the world premiere that night. We were seated in the centre of the Piccadilly Cinema about two-thirds the way back. We could see David and Amber down the front to the right.

The film started. About an hour in, you could have heard a pin drop, nobody was moving and I thought fuck everyone hates it. The film seemed to be even more handheld than I remembered. The camera moving all over the place. What were we thinking? Why did Warwick choose handheld when he knows? He knows. David is going to neuter us.

We couldn't have imagined the reception to the film once it finished. From everyone else but David. Where was David? David had vanished.

Fear and loathing, self-doubt set in. Handheld is good – what's wrong with handheld? There's nothing wrong with handheld. What would David know? Well, a lot actually. We won the Audience Award at Adelaide Film Festival. We were content with that – we had the audience on our side. Who needs David? We needed David. We wanted David. We craved David.

We all came back to Sydney and tried to return to normal life. In the office of the distributor, Footprint Films, our distribution manager Courtney Botfield said the office was crazy and the phones were ringing all day and requests flooding in. The film was gathering momentum. Chris Chamberlin, our beautiful publicist, told us that after a media screening in Sydney, a journalist came up to him and said – Chris, this is a really important film. Do you realise what an important film this is? Don't fuck it up, Chris. Chris, didn't fuck it up. Chris did a remarkable job and we mourn his absence from our lives, rest in peace you beautiful soul.

Roll forward to the day the review went to air. Chris tried to coax Amber into revealing what the scores were. We knew Margaret was onside but we were still on tenterhooks about David. Amber wouldn't give anything away, except to say she thought we would be happy. Happy!

I was in Alice Springs with Beck Cole, Warwick's partner, finishing off a documentary about the making of the film. We had a Margaret-and-David party at Beck's house with Warwick's mother, Freda, and Warwick and Beck's daughter Luka. We watched the show go to air and at some point there was screaming and jumping on couches. We rang Warwick who was in Perth doing media. The telecast in Perth was delayed because of the time difference, so he hadn't seen it. He was at the pub with some people, ran back to his hotel room and popped the telly on, waiting for the show to air. Later he told me he was slapping the TV. Who slaps TVs? Hmmm.

You know what it did for us, what it did for our film? It created its own media. We got media articles about the reviews and the scores – it snowballed and it kept the film in the news pages. It was the gift that kept on giving. It kept the film in the forefront of punters' minds. They kept going to the Nova. And the Dendy and the Luna Leederville. They kept going in droves because Margaret and David told them to. And then when we went to Cannes and Warwick won the Camera d'Or prize, it was back in the news again. Week after week.

For a tough little film like ours, this was an extraordinary reaction and so heart-warming for us, for the Aboriginal communities in Central Australia, for our young first-time actors, for the cause. The Cause. For budding young(ish) filmmakers all over Australia.

It's such a loss for today's filmmakers that they will never have this. They will always have to wonder what Margaret and David would have given them. Left wondering. We know. David even loved the handheld. He said something about an 'absolute object lesson'.

Thank you, Margaret and David, for your contribution to the success of our film, but more for your absolute object lesson in how to support, invigorate, challenge and inspire an entire nation's film culture.

Hon. Jay Weatherill,

a lawyer with an economics degree, was elected to parliament
in 2002. He held a range of senior Cabinet portfolios and was
elected South Australia's forty-fifth premier in 2014.
He is strong supporter of the arts.

fresh eyes

Jay Weatherill

'Oh, David!' For almost thirty years, those two words served as a signal that Margaret Pomeranz and David Stratton were about to have – on national television – an entertaining and good-natured barney about a just-released film.

I loved watching Margaret and David on SBS's *The Movie Show* and, later, on ABC's *At the Movies*. Like many Australians, I miss their banter and their often radically different takes on the films they reviewed.

Sometimes I came down on Margaret's side, sometimes David's. What they nearly always managed to do, however, was make me want to go to the cinema, see the movie in question and make up my own mind.

Margaret and David's hugely popular television show succeeded for a remarkably long time not just because they complemented one another, but because they were always genuine and generous. And I have seen these qualities, on a personal level, for many years.

I remember holidaying, with my family, in the Blue Mountains, near Sydney, and meeting up with David. We went bushwalking with his lovely wife Susie, while David entertained our two children with a showing of Bugs Bunny cartoons. We then enjoyed a superb meal and were all ushered into his private cinema, where we were treated to *What's Up, Doc?* – a Barbra Streisand classic. It was a beautifully curated evening of film that spoke to both generations. That is David – a super host.

As for Margaret, I have rarely met a more positive and engaging person. She has that unforgettable, unmistakable laugh. And it is impossible not to be infected by her love of life and of fine cinema. Like David, she has been an influential player in the Australian movie scene for many years, and her passion is undiminished.

It is always fun to spend time with Margaret and David because – quite apart from their unmatched knowledge of cinema – they really do love the medium and are passionate about its future. Even though they have been watching movies virtually all their lives and been heavily involved in the industry, they are remarkably open and unjaded. They are still moved and thrilled and stimulated by film, and that comes through clearly whenever they write or talk about cinema. Their ability to view cinema with a 'fresh eye' has, I believe, led to them being invited to be critics for various media outlets and jurors for numerous film festivals around the world.

Above all, Margaret and David are both champions of the Australian film industry and, specifically, the South Australian industry. By supporting our sector – and this, quite properly, does not always mean unalloyed praise of our films – they make it artistically and financially stronger. Few people better understand the economic, globalised and increasingly collaborative nature of modern cinema and, therefore, what a place like South Australia needs to do at the grass roots to maintain its reputation and technical capability.

I have especially appreciated the support they have given over the years to the Adelaide Film Festival. Through their advice they have made it a better program, and through their direct involvement they have lifted its profile. By serving as Festival jurors and by recording their television show at the AFF, they bolstered the national and international standing of the event.

I am really looking forward to seeing David's documentary, *Stories of Australian Cinema*, which has been supported through the Adelaide Film Festival Fund. I saw glimpses of the movie when it was shown as a work in progress in Adelaide in October 2016, and it is superb in its scope and insight. It made me realise how many great Australian films have been made and how few I have actually seen. It also reminds us of the power of cinema to portray Australia – its vernacular, its landscapes, its people – and project it boldly and truthfully to the world.

Margaret and David are great people and wonderful company. Their love of cinema is real, undiminished and contagious, and they have helped me and countless other Australians to understand the critical role film can play in telling our nation's stories and presenting our values. I am so very pleased that – in recognition of their passion, vision and support for the Australian screen industry – Margaret and David are the recipients of the 2017 Adelaide Film Festival Don Dunstan Award.

Sandy George

has tracked the Aussie film and television industry since
the beginning of time. She's been correspondent for
Screendaily.com, *Screen International*, film writer for
the *Australian*, and editor of *Encore*. She is currently
providing the industry with robust market intelligence on
financing via a partnership with Screen Australia.

margaret and david, the film business, film diversity and aussie film

Sandy George

THE NATURE OF MARGARET AND DAVID

For forty-four weeks of the year for twenty-eight years Margaret and David reviewed films together, first on *The Movie Show* on SBS then, after David was treated very disrespectfully by a new broom, on *At the Movies* on ABC. To the end they did it with an efficiency that was necessary: they only had half an hour to talk about four or five films about to hit cinemas for the first time and, in later years, one classic film.

They took film seriously and were very knowledgeable about it.

They had a reputation for having skirmishes. This meant the audience, watching from lounge chairs across

Australia, always felt a kind of delicious potential tinged with tension. They wanted them to squabble and knew there would be no backing down from either of them when they did. But they also knew it would be highly entertaining without turning ugly.

This is why David Tiley says of Margaret and David: 'They are the parents we all wish we had.' Apparently David Tiley had a turbulent childhood when with his parents. From his point of view, Margaret and David's modus operandi was a model for how families could have conflicts but resolve them nicely.

'They are very different people,' he says. 'He's a stiff older man and she's mischievous. They challenge each other but they enjoy it. They fight but they always remain affectionate with each other. The way they resolve their disagreements is comforting and it makes you feel safe in that environment. That's what is so utterly charming about them.'

David is editor of the online Australian film industry news service *Screenhub* and has written and script edited several productions, principally documentary. He's very interested in character.

'If you work in this industry and don't like conflict – can't go there yourself – you don't belong in film and television. If you run away from conflict in your life it can freeze your imagination on a deep level – unless you use your imagination to resolve it. On a philosophical level, drama is based on conflict. The basis of a dynamic journey is that the characters are going towards something, there are obstacles in the way, there's conflict … It's not just about what happens next.'

Given how keen Margaret and David are to lock horns, perhaps they missed their calling. Margaret describes David as a frustrated actor and she completed a one-year playwriting course at NIDA (the National Institute of Dramatic Art) and wrote drama and documentaries before joining SBS in 1980. On reflection no – they most definitely found their calling side by side discussing film and bickering.

In the early 1990s, David was offered the role of a villain in the Australian horror film Body Melt, *directed by Philip Brophy. The script was full of gruesome mutations. 'I would have had a very squishy fate if I'd agreed to be in it,' says David.*

'I seriously thought about saying yes. Cowardly, I decided no. I would have liked to be an actor but the life of an actor is perilous. I honestly don't know if I'd have had the guts. It's a brave thing because you never know when the next pay cheque is coming … Exposing yourself by playing different roles also takes courage.'

Margaret and David worked together for a few years prior to the 1986 launch of *The Movie Show*, she producing his movie introductions. They were politically aligned and got on well. The on-air partnership almost didn't happen. The plan was for Margaret to produce the new show, which they had devised together, not be the on-air 'talent'. Her hand was forced, she says, because he rejected every suggestion she came up with for a female co-host and the woman David proposed wasn't interested in the gig.

'He wanted an attractive shapely young woman who was working for *Cleo*,' says Margaret. 'After she said no – I don't think she saw herself on television – David said to me, "Why don't you do it?" ... I said no but Peter Barrett, then head of programming, said, "Yes, why don't you give it a go."' We did a couple of test reviews and the rest is history.'

Margaret's conversation is peppered with one-liners. She adds: 'He likes cool blondes and I was a feisty blonde ... David cried the day Grace Kelly married because he thought she'd wait for him.'

Margaret and David have very different personalities. There is no doubt that those differences, and the alternating fondness and irritation between them, fuelled their longevity. It's what they riffed off. People love talking about that aspect of them still.

'Oh, David, don't be *ridiculous!*' Margaret would say, a physical convulsion clearly communicating her exasperation. She: passionate, enthusiastic, up for anything, all-over-the-shop chaotic, liable to shriek at any moment.

'Margaret. I *really* don't know how you can say that,' David would say, the full weight of his superior knowledge behind him. He: disciplined, organised, articulate, eloquent, considered, with a good dollop of British reserve. (Margaret, Sydney-born, often uses the word 'anal' in relation to David, but it seems a bit mean.)

Margaret and David are Margaret Pomeranz and David Stratton of course. But in certain circles in Australia, great big overlapping circles, it is not necessary to use their last names, just as it's not necessary to use Madonna Louise Ciccone.

Madonna works just fine.

Their personal differences are also reflected in the style of their reviews. He's the professional critic with the vast knowledge and the academic and scholarly approach. It always seems like a checklist is lurking. If there were room on television for footnotes he probably would have used them.

David recently starred in the fabulous feature-length documentary *David Stratton's A Cinematic Life* (2017), in which he explores the circumstances around some of his favourite Aussie films. During the film he pulls out from a two-ring folder a review he wrote of the Australian film *The Overlanders* (1946). It's a short, straightforward assessment, handwritten on an A4 sheet of paper and illustrated with a picture from the film. It records when and where he saw it. It's not surprising that he wrote it when he was seven years old, but it is a wee bit shocking that his habit of reviewing films took hold around then and persisted – and that the review is not packed away in a dusty box under the house but in a line-up of similar folders, each labelled by year, on a shelf in his home office.

David's love of film is of obsession proportions. At the time of filming, he had seen – and carefully recorded that he'd seen – 25,254 different films. The expectation that he would join the family grocery business in the south-east of England was never going to happen.

He'd earned his film stripes long before *The Movie Show*, having spent eighteen years as director of the Sydney Film Festival (SFF). He got the gig three years after arriving in Australia in 1963 as a ten-pound Pom and his book *I Peed on Fellini* details how confidently he embraced the role and the adventures he had along the way. (It also tells how, when David was a toddler, the celebrated actor Laurence Olivier accidentally knocked him over, picked him up and planted a kiss on his head before handing him back to his mother.) During the six years before the launch of the new show, David worked as feature film consultant for the then newly established multicultural broadcaster and for two of those years had been reviewing for LA-based industry trade magazine *Variety*. His film knowledge was extraordinary. He'd also begun serving on international film festival juries by then.

Margaret is the pop critic in comparison. Her approach feels more accessible, personal, emotional, unpredictable. She lets whatever she thinks all hang out, and seems more open to supporting new ways of telling stories and filmmaking that takes risks.

'I reckon I'm one of the luckiest people in the world to have had a personal and professional relationship with David,' she says. 'He gave me credibility as a critic by being willing to sit next to me. My credibility comes as a result of his endorsement.'

Margaret studied economics at Sydney University and German and psychology at Macquarie University and, as part of qualifying as a teacher, worked in country New South Wales for three years. She headed to Vienna to improve her language skills, returned to Sydney for more study with the intention of returning to Europe, but met

Dutch migrant Hans Pomeranz, founder of the legendary Sydney post-production facility, Spectrum Films. They married in 1971 just as Australian feature film production blossomed and his love of cinema infected her. Their son Josh now runs Spectrum; their other son Felix works in film visual effects. Margaret doesn't have grandchildren but wishes she did. Hans died in 2007.

Margaret undoubtedly found her own path – and in a way that meant she and David didn't occupy the same space.

'The thing about Margaret is that she's very open,' says Australian filmmaker Sue Brooks, who directed *Japanese Story* (2003) and wrote and directed *Looking for Grace* (2015). 'From a filmmaker's point of view that's a wonderful audience to have. If you're showing someone a film that you hope will shock, surprise, amuse or move an audience, they need to have genuine warmth in order to have the capacity to respond. I'm overwhelmed by his knowledge but I'm delighted by her capacity to be open. Think about how many films she's watched over the years and she's still not cynical.'

It is surprising to hear Margaret say that David taught her to be positive. She recalls how, before *The Movie Show* was launched, a discussion about the Australian film *The Empty Beach* was a turning point for her.

'I was scathing and David was much more generous,' she says. 'I started to look more at the whole. I loved film but I'd only see one a week. I wasn't a film critic and it was a learning curve and an eye opener to suddenly be seeing six, seven, eight films a week. When you see that many you get more discerning about the art, the craft, what you like.'

Many say that Margaret and David taught them and Australia how to talk about film. The pair encourages appreciation of film and makes it very clear that any opinion has validity. They also set the bar high because they are both good people who believe in a fair society.

'The remarkable thing about our on-screen and personal relationship is that there has not been a single falling out in all those years,' says Margaret. 'David didn't like it when I didn't use an interview that he'd recorded in Cannes with the actor Leo McKern but it was recorded on the beach and I couldn't understand a word of it because of the wind. It wasn't personal. He was also upset with me on the stance I took on Romper Stomper *(1992) – I think he was disappointed in me.' Margaret reviewed the Australian film in line with the show's usual style while making it clear that watching it wasn't a pleasant experience: 'It is relentlessly psychologically violent, almost nauseatingly so on occasion, however it is one of the*

finest films to be made in this country in recent years.' When she threw to David he explained that he couldn't support it because it fell into the trap of celebrating racially motivated violence. After some discussion between them he famously refused to rate the film. Margaret gave it four-and-a-half stars. 'With racism on the march again all over the world, this is a dangerous film,' he said. His behaviour brought the film a lot of attention. During their last year on air both Margaret and David decided not to review Wolf Creek 2 *(2013) as it was released while* At the Movies *was off-air. When the show returned, it was a busy week for new releases – and they both felt uncomfortable about the amount of violence it contained. Margaret likes to say she's not into 'torture porn'. Again it gave the film a lot of oxygen. Both have been fervent anti-censorship campaigners.*

'There's a whole range of responses you have to watching a film,' says Sue. 'What they did reflected that sort of energy. A long review in a newspaper can feel like a dead piece of description but on television you get a sense of all the different layers of how a film impacts an audience. They conveyed why we see films and why we read books: because they're good for the soul and they're full of ideas and they jostle with your values.

'Their whole way of chatting was familiar. It was the

same way you'd talk to your friends about film. They were like trusted friends.'

On the other hand, and as Margaret herself says, there is no comparison between four minutes of television and a well thought through 1500-word review in print: 'Television is a different beast. It's superficial. When I first started the show not many films released each week. But there's been an explosion. How to fit all the films in was always the challenge. I was never averse to a 90-second encapsulation but David was never keen.'

Yet people hung on to what she and David said despite their reviews being bite-sized because they had good taste and took the trouble to honour the work in a way that enriched the experience of movie-going.

Being able to show film clips was a bonus. Besides being entertaining, they help viewers decide if something might suit their taste and be worth taking a risk on.

'For a long time they guided my movie-going, at least insofar as films not to be missed and absolute duds were concerned,' says Dorothy, in her 70s. 'You have to have some respect for the knowledge gained from watching a lifetime of films. And the fact that they were not on commercial television increased their credibility for me.' Says her husband, Ron: 'It was a useful way of keeping tabs on what might be worth seeing — and learning

a bit of cinematic history from David. He was a polished performer but I'd get a bit irritated by Margaret's excessive use of "you know" when speaking off the cuff.' Says their daughter Jessica, 30s: 'I must confess to a soft spot for David; he's such a grumpy father figure. I took his recommendations more seriously than Margaret's. She liked more of the films.'

Time and time again, and still, it is implied that Margaret and David have very different taste in film. But do they? Differences are least evident in their most beloved contemporary films but he certainly gets more of a kick out of classic cinema and Margaret is generally not amused by the British sense of humour that he so loves.

The notion that they fundamentally disagree became widespread because it made the news when they did disagree, says David. Margaret says it's less that they have different taste and more that they can – and do – appreciate the same films for different reasons.

'I love the narrative aspects and great dialogue. I think David does too but he has more of an overview. And he loves the perfect frame.'

David doesn't hesitate when asked what the best films have in common: 'Emotion. If a film lacks emotion to take you into it, to affect and move you, then it's dead ... Most of the great films I would place high in my pantheon reflect this strongly. Even with comedy, unless there is a realistic base to the film, it's not going to work.'

But does he include the kind of emotion that's triggered when a moment in a horror film makes you jump out of your cinema seat – or hold onto it in the case of a car chase in a thriller? What about tent-pole movies, the ones that rake in billions of dollars worldwide for the Hollywood studios?

'Those tent poles don't have emotion,' he says, with some disdain. 'Maybe once upon a time: *Spartacus* (1960) was full of emotion, that's what made it so good ... Characters that you care about: that's the main thing a film needs. You have to care what happens to them.'

Kirk Douglas played the gladiator Spartacus. It does cross the mind that David's taste is stuck in the past but it could be that he has been watching films for longer than most and has a memory so flawless that he can pull out perfect examples to illustrate whatever he's saying.

When Margaret is asked what films particularly appeal to her she responds: 'When the experience of watching them makes me come out feeling transformed in some way. Maybe it's only in a minor way. Not a lot of films do that, but some do.'

She uses *Housekeeping* (1987) as an example. Scottish director Bill Forsyth, who won BAFTAs for directing *Local Hero* and writing *Gregory's Girl*, filmed the US comedy drama in Canada. Two teenage sisters and the eccentric aunt who looks after them are the characters at its core.

'I felt that it endorsed difference in a really beautiful way,' she says. The other film that springs to her mind is *Samson & Delilah* (2009), Warwick Thornton's feature film debut as a writer, director and cinematographer. It was filmed in Central Australia and won the Camera d'Or at the Cannes Film Festival.

'Warwick says in David's documentary (*David Stratton's A Cinematic Life*) that he was unable to kill off Samson and Delilah because they had become irrepressible. I loved the compassion he had for those two characters. The film is mind-blowingly compassionate.'

Margaret and David's on-air relationship ended with the December 2014 broadcast of the final episode of *At the Movies*. They still talk to each other every couple of days and Margaret confesses that she still feels sad that they're not working together.

This is despite her having a new partner-in-film, television critic and actor Graeme Blundell. His acting career really kicked off with the Alvin Purple comedies of the 1970s. He played the irresistible-to-women title character.

Margaret and Graeme have appeared on Foxtel since April 2015, first as the hosts of *Screen*, which reviewed film, television and online content, but now as part of a bigger on-air team on *Stage & Screen*, which also covers theatre, music, visual arts and so on. Margaret says she covers two or three films a week and couldn't go back to five or six. She also introduces movies.

Margaret says David had wanted to stop doing *At the Movies* at the 25-year mark. There were a lot of celebrations at that time including an exhibition at ACMI in Melbourne. She persuaded him otherwise: 'He lives out of town and wasn't enjoying having to schlep in for *Spiderman 6*.

'It's lucky we've never fancied each other,' she says suddenly, with that laugh of hers.

David lives in the Blue Mountains with his wife Susie and is very close to her son Ben. He and his first wife Margaret have two children, Mary and Giles, as well as grandchildren.

Helen, sixties, has learned a lot in the last year about where to access movies after deciding to watch all those that received five stars from either Margaret or David. Good Night, and Good Luck, Brokeback Mountain, Samson & Delilah, No Country for Old Men, A Separation *and* Amour *got five stars from both of them while they were on* At the Movies. *David gave five stars to an additional eleven films, all of which got four or four-and-a-half stars from Margaret. She gave five stars to an additional fifteen films – David gave four or four-and-a-half stars to these films with the exception of* Last Days, The Tree of Life *and* Melancholia. *SBS has a record of which films got five stars but not who gave them five stars.*

MARGARET AND DAVID'S IMPACT ON THE BUSINESS

There was about $1.26 billion spent on movie tickets in Australia in 2016. This represents about 90 million ticket sales.

Every one of the ten biggest hits of the year (*Finding Dory, Deadpool, Rogue One: A Star Wars Story, Suicide Squad, Captain America: Civil War, Fantastic Beasts and Where to Find Them, Star Wars: The Force Awakens, The Jungle Book, Batman v Superman: Dawn of Justice* and *The Secret Life of Pets*), which attracted nearly one-third of all that box office revenue, were either animations, sequels or spin-offs, or films featuring superheroes or comic book characters. Some had a foot in two of these camps. All were made with families, young adults or very broad audiences in mind.

'Blockbusters are getting a bigger and bigger share of revenue and attention,' says Margaret. 'Humans have a herd mentality. It's going to continue.

'I do feel that the cost of filmmaking has become obscene. There was a healthy balance between art and commerce thirty years ago but now the pendulum has swung to the commercial side ... I got very angry at (filmmaker) George Lucas for those crappy, badly written *Star Wars* films that rode on the coat-tails of the magic of earlier times.'

Frankly, the popularity of *Star Wars* and of the ten runaway-train movies named above was not affected one iota by whether people saw Margaret and David talking about them. But the contraction of the pair's reach and impact has made life in Australia more difficult for foreign-language films, independent Australian films (i.e. not *Mad Max: Fury Road*, which is Hollywood backed) and independent films from elsewhere too. These films are so wildly diverse that it's very difficult to describe them. It might be clearer to say what they're not: films made with huge production and marketing budgets. They include films that are thoughtful, confronting, based on true stories. Some are windows on to different worlds. Many are damn fine films with great artistic merit.

They depend on critical review rather than being critic proof.

'Lots of films arrive with nothing more than a popcorn and a populist reason for being,' says Mike Baard, managing director of Universal Pictures Australasia, distributor of *The Secret Life of Pets*, one of the ten big hits. 'There are other films that have met with acclaim, bring with them a particular point of view and make an incredibly smart statement about the world we live in. Margaret and David were able to explain why a film was relevant and contextualise its message.'

Distributors as a group bemoan the disappearance of *At the Movies* because Australia's king and queen of film criticism have a unique ability to entice people to leave their homes and see films in cinemas.

Palace Films general manager Nic Whatson: 'It has placed incredible pressure on a distributor's ability to cut through and get visibility for those films ... The beautiful thing about Margaret and David is that they embraced films that took risks.'

Entertainment One managing director of film for the Asia–Pacific Troy Lum (*La La Land*): 'We used to rely on Margaret and David. If they gave a film a good review it would be broadcast to literally hundreds of thousands of people and that would make it viable. Them not being on the scene means it is very hard to get that kind of exposure any more.'

Troy was one of the founders of the art-house distribution company Hopscotch, since subsumed into the international company eOne Entertainment. As a result he now has access to films with much broader appeal.

Madman Entertainment joint founder/managing director

Paul Wiegard (*Hunt for the Wilderpeople*): 'There is no question that they had a dedicated audience. There would not be a distributor out there that wouldn't love both of them giving a film four or five stars – or embrace one lauding the filmmaker's endeavours and the other being completely diametrically opposed. In this business we hate indifference and love polarity. If they really didn't like a film they'd probably not choose to review it at all and I valued that – not that we had many films that fell into that category!'

Paul is quick to note that, from the industry's point of view, Margaret and David are still very present. It's not like they've retired or morphed into winemakers or opted for some other sea change. David continues to review for the *Australian* as he has for nearly thirty years and, as mentioned, Margaret is on Foxtel. But the reality is that both are less visible now.

David has been running a history of film course through the Continuing Education program of Sydney University since 1990. The first ran for five years, the next for ten, and he might extend the current one to fifteen years. 'When I think of the amount of time I spend researching compared to the amount of money I'm paid it doesn't compute,' he says. 'But the incredible pleasure it gives me is beyond recompense. It's wonderful.'

David had no formal education beyond school.

'Their loss is felt more deeply because there is less reviewing occurring in mainstream media, including print media,' says Tracey Mair, one of the busiest and most established independent publicists in the film business. Like many, including Margaret and David, she mentions that Fairfax Media has reduced its review and reviewer numbers and says that newspapers generally give less space to film – in particular to small, important and intriguing films.

'Authoritative and intelligent criticism that develops a deep understanding of and love for screen culture is now seriously lacking.'

But isn't there an army of bloggers and podcasters out there making up for their free-to-air absence? 'Yes but it takes fifty times the work [to reach them] and you need fifty times the coverage for the same impact,' she says. 'Plus a lot of smaller outlets would take their lead from Margaret and David. They were so influential. There's no one to quote any more on posters or other marketing materials.'

She laughs after adding: 'And no one to quote at the dinner table.'

Some regard the end of *At the Movies* as a sign of the times. 'You sadly have to accept that film criticism as a discipline has massively diminished in favour of the aggregated voice of popular opinion,' says Universal's Mike Baard. 'The era of the Pauline Kaels and the Roger Eberts (prominent US critics) is over and there has not been an equivalent rise. Sites such as Rotten Tomatoes aggregate the opinion and sentiment of all critics.

'They (Margaret and David) stayed relevant longer than most and went out without losing their cachet. But their audience was educated, interested in culture, over forty, generally well off. It's a fact that the young filmgoer, the lover of blockbusters above all else, well, they always gathered elsewhere.'

When David is asked what being a celebrity is like he modifies the question before answering: he's a mini-celebrity he says.

'People think they know you because they see you on television every week. They are always friendly. Sometimes they're mildly intimate. At 5 pm one day in George Street in Sydney a quite attractive young woman grabbed me on the bum.'

Then she ran away.

'It (the absence of *At the Movies*) has left a hole in terms of film reviews but did the show come to an end of its life because the need for a program just on film reviewing has come to an end of its life?' asks producer Chris Brown in a way that indicates it's a rhetorical question. Chris has produced films in the US, New Zealand and Australia, including *The Proposition* (2005), *Daybreakers* (2009) and *The Railway Man* (2013).

'There's more film content in other television programs now. People can go online and find video interviews with the directors. There's easy access to the trades.'

It is true that a variety of morning, chat and lifestyle programs cover films – even if they do focus on high-profile films and celebrity interviews – and that there has been a gargantuan increase in the accessibility of film information from amateurs and professionals. It's also easier to reach people directly: cinema chains now have flourishing film clubs that deliver data on age, gender, location and film preferences; and niche audiences can be efficiently reached with digital advertising.

But actually there's something much bigger at stake here than the nature of the film criticism changing, and that's the survival of film diversity in cinemas.

Independent film distribution is a risky business and, although most company executives love cinema from the bottom of their hearts, they don't run charities. And the saying 'you have to spend money to make money' holds true big time for film.

Distributors can pay up to $1.5 million for the

Australian and New Zealand rights to a film – the minimum is probably about $100,000. On top of that, they might spend $200,000 to $2 million on marketing. They get all this money back but only if the film earns enough to cover it. And therein lies the risk. Distributors get a cut of the cinema ticket revenue – if they successfully persuade cinemas for a spot in their schedules – but only once the cinemas have taken as much as sixty-five per cent. Distributors also get revenue or commissions from DVD, television, video-on-demand, airlines and so on but how a film performs in cinemas in the first instance has a big flow-on affect through all the other platforms. (The model for the studios is different because of their vertical integration.)

The thing about Margaret and David is that they take the junk-food films and commercially risky films – and everything in between – with the same level of earnestness. If the loss of the partnership means fewer of the risky films are picked up by the distributors, whining about great films losing their support becomes redundant because the films aren't going to make it to Australia's shores! Instead, as Margaret suggests, the rush for revenue will tip the scales even further towards the films that make all the noise and take up all the space with their bells and whistles.

'It hasn't affected Palace's acquisition of foreign-language and quality films,' says Palace Films' Nic Whatson, but he knows some distributors have backed off. Every distributor has different circumstances and strategies. Nic is advantaged by the existence of Palace Cinemas – although the sister company rarely keeps a Palace film on screen if that film is grossing less than some other distributor's, he says.

Such films as *The Lives of Others* (2006, Margaret five stars, David four) and *Pan's Labyrinth* (2006, Margaret and David both four-and-a-half) attracted many fans but now foreign-language films are particularly vulnerable. eOne's Troy Lum used to release six or seven a year but *Incendies* (2010, Margaret three stars, David four), six years ago, was the last. David described *Incendies* as 'utterly gripping in its depiction of the evils of civil war and fundamentalism'; Margaret thought it a bit heavy-handed.

'The world of cinema has shifted towards the big spectacle,' says Troy. Underlying his point is the fact that *Incendies* director Denis Villeneuvre's most recent film is *Blade Runner 2049* (2017).

'It (the disappearance of *At the Movies*) has sounded the death knell for art cinema,' he says. It is such a big statement. Really? 'Yes. It's been a confluence of things.

There's a film festival every week and that's where people get their art-house fix and that does a lot to kill off commercial releases. People's taste has moved on from foreign language and art-house films to TV. Young audiences have not been developed in the art-house space. University students used to go to art-house films, but not any more – and it's those original university students who are still going.

'I couldn't start a company like Hopscotch now. Margaret and David's interest in art-house film definitely helped make Australia one of biggest art-house markets in the world. Without a doubt we can't afford to buy that kind of cinema and distribute it here. I'm talking about great, audacious, exciting cinema.'

'David and Margaret. D&M. Deep and meaningful. Getting to the heart of the minutiae of being human through the medium of film.' Matt, forties, used to say that to himself when he watched the pair on television.

Cinema didn't become spectacle overnight. Blockbusters barged in decades ago. Look back at the top ten films at the cinema twenty years ago and there's the first *Men in Black*, the second *Jurassic Park* film, and movies in the *Batman* and *Star Wars* series.

But also in the top ten are dramas and comedies containing real or real-ish people and scenarios. There's

Bean, *The Full Monty*, *My Best Friend's Wedding*, *Jerry Maguire*, *Liar Liar* and *Romeo + Juliet* – although it's reality is rather heightened and Shakespeare is one of the world's most resilient franchises.

These days mid-budget dramas and films with any sense of believability to them (even when they've got a thick coating of entertainment value) rarely get the very biggest audiences. Who knows whether it's a lack of marketing or a shift in taste and fashion, but it's a vicious circle. As for the brave, bold, challenging films: good luck finding them in the commercial space outside the inner city.

The Internet means it has never been easier to access films of any kind from anywhere but the experience someone gets while sitting on their own comfy lounge bears no comparison to the thrill of being blown away in front of a big screen, in the dark, at one with the rest of the audience. It can be an intense experience to be in the shoes of a character going through extremes of emotion in such an environment.

Giving Margaret and David awards for their long service is more appropriate than cursing them for any of this of course. They are both in their seventies now; they can't live on forever as the Australian desert landscape that features so often in Australian films can.

Margaret was made a Member of the Order of Australia in 2005 for service to the film industry as a critic and reviewer, promoter of Australian content and advocate for freedom of expression in film. Ten years later David won the same award. By then he was already a recipient of the Raymond Longford Award and the Charles Chauvel Award. He is an Honorary Doctor of Letters (University of Sydney and Macquarie University) and a Commander of the Order of Arts and Letters (France).

Margaret still feels she let people down by leaving the ABC: 'We are greeted constantly by people in the street who say 'we don't know what to see anymore'. We were a buyers' guide to the cinema. We reached 700,000 people every week on all the different platforms; that's 700,000 people focused on cinema.'

She didn't have a choice. David pulled the plug for several reasons. He felt he was getting stale, for example. 'Margaret wasn't. She is always perky and bright. Another reason is that we had to spend our time reviewing awful films,' he says. 'Worse, we had to spend time watching them. Mainstream American cinema has never been worse.'

What he says next indicates that films and filmmakers everywhere have to take some responsibility for the changing environment.

'There are some very very fine American independent films that come out around Oscar time but overall American cinema is almost pathetically dreadful. Unfortunately, more than that, European cinema is a pale shadow of what it was years ago.'

David says 'amazing' films emerged from France, Italy, Sweden, Hungary and Poland in the 1960s. Federico Fellini's *La Dolce Vita* and Luchino Visconti's *Rocco and His Brothers* (Italy), François Truffaut's *Shoot the Piano Player* and Jacques Demy's *Lola* (France) all came out in 1960. Another film from that year, Vittorio De Sica's *Two Women*, earned Sophia Loren the Academy Award for best actress, the first time an acting Oscar had gone to a performance not in English.

'It was an extraordinary time. Only occasionally do films of that quality now emerge,' he says, naming Asghar Farhadi from Iran and Kenneth Lonergan as outstanding contemporary directors. 'I look at the French Film Festival program and there's nothing much I want to see. Maybe it's because I'm getting older and I look back with ... no, no I don't look back with nostalgia, I look back with awe at the fifties and sixties and also the seventies.'

Does he have a theory on the reason? 'Maybe the great directors have died or retired and the ones who have taken their place don't aspire so high, or are lazy. I don't know. Films reflect the time and place they're made. Always. They are a mirror. Life was getting better in Europe in the sixties, fifteen years after a very destructive war. Maybe the world is in a bad state now.

'I love cinema and feel very disappointed by this.'

Then he turns his attention to Australia: 'In the seventies we had Peter Weir, Gillian Armstrong, Fred Schepisi, Paul Cox, Bruce Beresford at his best. Where are the successes of today? There's Rolf de Heer and David Michôd.'

David's sentiment echoes something Troy said a week earlier: 'Don't you look at the Cannes competition lineup and think "Not those old dudes again!"? Where are the new great filmmakers? Cinema hasn't moved on.'

Does David think that quality cinema might emerge as a result of the raging against US president Donald Trump? 'It will need courage and the attitude of a Robert Altman or a Stanley Kubrick or a young Woody Allen. It's perfectly possible.'

Many describe film as the art form of the twentieth century. It is chilling to think that the current century might well see its demise.

Suggesting such a thing might seem sensationalist but the studios' overwhelming focus on brand exploitation has to end in audience fatigue. Attendance numbers are already flat. The rise of television drama is due to its originality, freshness and diversity but the studios are ignoring that. Instead, they seem to think the effort being put into shrinking the theatrical window – that is, getting films onto other platforms more quickly after a cinema season – is the best way to increase revenue. Giving cinemas much less exclusive access to films will be great for some, parents of young families for example, but it will weaken the important link between cinema and the big screen.

Here's a thought: while Hollywood is having a reboot, maybe it's the perfect time for independent filmmakers and small national film industries such as Australia's to shine.

David's favourite film is Singin' in the Rain *(1952). His Australian favourite is* Newsfront *(1978). Margaret's favourite film is* Nashville *(1975). Her Australian favourite is ... 'I hate that question, I hate it. I think* Animal Kingdom *(2010) is stunning.* Samson & Delilah *is a knockout. If I had to choose one I'd say* Samson & Delilah *but there are zillions of others. I loved* Priscilla *(1994). I'll never forget (the director) Stephan Elliott walking down the front to introduce the film. He said, "When I was a little kid I just wanted the curtains to go wider, and wider, and wider." It was one of the most exhilarating evenings at the cinema. And really moving.'*

MARGARET AND DAVID AND AUSTRALIAN FILMS

Sometimes Australian films could be tricky terrain for Margaret and David.

'We were doing interviews with Australian filmmakers and trying not to be friends with them, but it's impossible,' says Margaret. 'I have friends who are filmmakers and when I have to see their films I hope and pray that I'm going to like them.' She pauses. 'I have always been kind to Australian films because I'm such a wimp.' But she also says this: 'I would rather see a mediocre film from Australia with my landscapes, my culture, my accent, then a mediocre international film ... I get moved and excited by Australian cinema when I see the montage at the annual AACTA Awards.'

As one distributor said, one way the pair went above and beyond for Australian films was how carefully they chose their words when one fell short.

'With a Harry Potter film it doesn't matter what people think of it; it is still going to do business,' says Seph McKenna, head of Australian production at Roadshow Films, one of the most important distributors of mainstream Australian films. 'But if they agreed with each other that *Bran Nue Dae* or *Beautiful Kate* or *Red Dog* were good, it made a huge difference. Margaret gave *Red Dog* four stars but she was seen as soft on Australian films. When David gave it four-and-a-half stars: boom! It was so legitimising, a huge driver of the initial business. It was the kindling on the fire of word of mouth.

'I miss having allies in the field. They could amplify the buzz around new talent or a new film they loved and nothing has filled the gap. It doesn't change what we do but we have lost a tool for doing it.'

It doesn't help Australian film that more people now get their film information from abroad. Writers and editors on offshore newspapers and websites don't have an understanding of and connection to Australian films in the way Australians do.

It also doesn't help that some Australian critics see reviewing local films as a blood sport. Many have no idea that it is a condition of financing through the main government agency that the films have to be released in cinemas whether they live up to their promise or not. That said a critic's first responsibility should be to his or her audience.

Margaret and David are cognisant of the great big dreams of the filmmakers, the immense challenge of making great cinema, and just how many people do their darnedest to make a film special.

They actively engage in talking about the narrative, the

history of the production, what the filmmaker was trying to achieve, and how the film affected them; they don't engage in reductive talk such as 'this is good', 'this is bad', 'see this', 'don't see that'.

'I moved into a share house when I first came to Australia from the US in 2006,' says Seph McKenna. 'My artistically switched-on PhD-in-psychotherapy roommate said, 'You work in the movies, you've got to watch Margaret and David.' We had one television and no wifi, and the four of us we would sit in the cold living room and watch together. It was the best share-house experience you could imagine. It was similar to the US show Siskel & Ebert *in that it had two hosts at each other's throats. Gene Siskel had died of a brain tumour by then. If anything, Margaret and David had more personality. I went off shaky cameras for years and wouldn't have thought to if not for David. It was interesting to hear Margaret talking up Australian films because you didn't have to be patriotic about local films in the US.'*

David wrote reviews for the extremely influential LA-based magazine *Variety* for twenty years up to 2003. He did this while attending festivals across the world or, in the case of some homegrown films, in Australia. These reviews could make or break a film – or cement or destroy a reputation – because film buyers read them.

'I never gave a glowing review to something that didn't

deserve it,' says David, 'but knowing how important a *Variety* review is, I sometimes went out of my way not to review a film.'

Instead he would suggest to the filmmakers that they show a print to a *Variety* reviewer in another part of the world – the policy once was to review all the films that came onto the magazine's radar via film festivals or a commercial release. Sometimes Todd McCarthy, chief film critic at *Variety* for much of the time David was there, would review an Australian film himself so that it got an outsiders' perspective.

Filmmakers would sometimes do some manipulating of their own. Says David: 'If the producers or the distributor had screened *Muriel's Wedding* (1994) in Sydney before it premiered in Cannes, I would have reviewed it, but they didn't. Todd hated it. I think PJ [the director P.J. Hogan] thought I'd written the review.'

Todd's 1994 review opens with '*Muriel's Wedding* is an aesthetically crude ugly-duckling fantasy shrewdly designed as a lowbrow audience pleaser'. He said it was likely to do good business, at least in English-language territories, with young women as the target audience. In Australia it captured the nation but *Variety* was principally concerned with the business a film would do in the US.

Todd McCarthy says in *David Stratton's A Cinematic Life*

that no other Australian critic is as well known outside Australia. He also says, with a mischievous smile: 'I wouldn't discount also his look because David was instantly identifiable: the white hair, the white beard and kind of the same suit most of the time.'

Sophie, twenties, jokes that her grandmother ended up in a nursing home when she was in her eighties because of Margaret and David. Actually she fell off the back step at Sophie's parents' place, suffered consequences from the fall and didn't recover enough to return to her own home. She'd been walking around in the city all day after going in to see the film that one of them had recommended. Sophie often watched At the Movies *with her grandmother.*

Asked what he'd do to improve Australian films David says: 'The industry is probably getting as much financial support as you could expect but it would be wonderful if films had decent marketing and promotional budgets. Time and time again on television we would talk about an Australian film and people would say they hadn't heard of it.'

But are there aspects of the filmmaking that can be improved? The strength of a film can be boiled down to the script, he says. Good scripts are dependent on scriptwriters having ideas and stories they really want to tell, not whether they have graduated from a course on screenwriting.

'Some of the best films have been made without that kind of tutelage,' he says. 'Peter Weir didn't go to film school; he learned his craft in a junior role at Channel Seven. Film is a collaborative art – and his films were written by or with very good writers – but the pattern is that they were stories he *had* to tell.

'There are more Australian films that are of high quality and didn't find a large audience than disappointing films that did,' says David. Films like *Breaker Morant* (1980), *Gallipoli* (1981), *Strictly Ballroom* (1992) and *Lantana* (2001) straddle popularity and excellence, but there are many others.

'There was a time in the seventies in the wake of *Picnic at Hanging Rock* (1975) and *My Brilliant Career* (1979) and others when Australian films were really embraced by Australians. People would look forward to the next one coming out and there was a real feeling of pride and affection for the mostly wonderful films made then. That bubble burst with the introduction of the (tax incentive) 10BA. Vast numbers of mediocre films came out, dramatically changing the proportion of good to disappointing films. That did a lot of damage to the trust and interest audiences had. Now local audiences take films on a one-by-one basis.

'The regular loyal audience that will go out and see Australian films tends to be an older audience and probably an educated audience but they won't necessarily go and see a sci-fi film such as *Predestination* (2014) or a horror film such as *The Babadook* (2014) and that's a shame. They're superb films, both of them.'

Brett, fifties, once found himself standing at a cinema urinal next to David. 'The experience has eclipsed all memory of who I was there with or what film I'd just seen but I feel like it was a shitty Australian film'. He remembers having a chuckle when he learned that David's autobiography was titled I Peed on Fellini *(2008). David has also written two books on Australian film,* The Last New Wave *(1980) and* The Avocado Plantation *(1990). Margaret has written a cookbook,* Let's Eat *(2017), with her daughter-in-law Philippa Whitfield Pomeranz.*

Margaret believes Australians want to like homegrown films but they also want to have a good time at the cinema. They loved *Strictly Ballroom* (1992), *The Adventures of Priscilla, Queen of the Desert* (1994) and the other comedies in the 1990s that celebrated quirkiness, but they lost interest when the films took a serious turn.

'People don't want to have to work at seeing films or be disturbed by them,' she says. 'Part of cinema's role is to entertain. People want to get away from hardship and dreariness.'

Like David, Margaret mentions script: 'We export

cinematographers and directors all over the world but I don't know if we've exported too many film writers. The Americans are so good at it and Britain too, where university drama societies spawned so many writers. I think our scripts are improving. Look at Luke Davies, who wrote *Lion*, a scriptwriter, a poet and a novelist.'

It sounds absurd to say it but grief seems to underpin what some fans wrote in their farewell comments on the At the Movies *website: it was like two of their dearest friends were being wrenched from their lives.*

'Last night we showed *Zach's Ceremony* and the cinema was filled with young people black and white,' says Tracey Mair. The Australian documentary is about a young man caught between the pressures and temptations of the modern world, the obligations of his ancient culture and the expectations of his father.

'We went out of our way to reach them, a lot of work if you don't have vast sums of money, and every one left saying they would tell their friends about the film,' she says. 'I think young people are seriously interested in cinema. Not all of them just love two-minute clips on YouTube.

'I profoundly believe that cinema can change the world for the better and can create deeper understanding between human beings. It's a joyous thing to be in a cinema full of people watching a film that prompts them to think about who they are and how they move through the world. As a society we need to give people that experience.'

Thank you Margaret and David for guiding our critical engagement with film for so many years and with so much love and care. The future is unpredictable and we don't know who or what will light the path for new generations but we hope it is not just algorithms.

'I thought one of us should have died in those chairs –
preferably him,' says Margaret. In other words, die on air.
She seems to be only half joking and punctuates her words with
that laugh, the laugh of a million durries. 'I've smoked forever
and still do,' she says. 'David absolutely hates it.'

Jan Chapman, AO

has produced some of Australia's most critically successful and
popular films including AFI, AACTA and Academy Award®
winners, as well as Caméra d'Or recipient *Love Serenade* (1996)
and the multi award-winning *Bright Star* (2009),
nominated for the Palme d'Or.

Jan was executive producer of Australian films *Somersault*
(2004) and *Suburban Mayhem* (2006), both of which were
selected for Un Certain Regard at Cannes and the Toronto
International Film Festival, and the Sundance sensation
The Babadook (2014), which won three AACTA Awards
including Best Film.

giving life

Jan Chapman

From the time I first began producing feature films Margaret and David were a pivotal part of the process. They gave your film a life.

I remember the thrill of viewing their review of the first one on *The Movie Show* in 1992, the Gillian Armstrong directed *The Last Days of Chez Nous*. It felt like you really *had* made a feature film if it was reviewed by Margaret and David.

And the following year their five-star reviews for *The Piano* followed the joy of having Jane Campion and our cast interviewed by them at the Cannes film festival when we were so amazed to share the prize of the Palme D'Or.

I came to realise what a pleasure it was to see them at

these festivals over the years, among our long rounds of press and publicity and off in the distance interviewing some greatly admired director or actor. It made us feel like we had access to these artists too.

When director Ray Lawrence and I ran into them at the airport after our closing night gala screening of *Lantana* at Toronto, just days after September 11, it was a particular kind of solace having shared what Margaret called 'the sadness of the world' in the confines of a film festival, which none of us could leave.

Margaret and David enabled us all to believe in our Australian film industry. In many ways they actually created it. With their serious analysis of the work and their passionate commitment they made us all feel a credibility, a belief in our films in the context of a world of cinema.

And all this in such an entertaining presentation. You made sure you never missed a show so that you could argue or agree with friends and fellow filmmakers about their opinions. It was the starting point of the discussion.

And they're still supporting our industry with reviews and presentations and retrospectives and public appearances. They separately hosted Q and As after screenings of our more recent film, Simon Stone's *The Daughter*, as they have for many other filmmakers, probing the process and aiding audiences in their appreciation of the work.

I've watched so many people approach Margaret Pomeranz and David Stratton like esteemed but familiar friends and be greeted with generosity.

They have given the Australian film industry a personality and fostered a cohesion among our various styles and approaches and a greater respect for each other out of our mutual appreciation and affection for them and for the significance they gave to our work.

Thank you, Margaret. Thank you, David.

Andrew Bovell

is a playwright and screenwriter and screenwriter and
recipient of the 2015 Don Dunstan Award and the 2017
Patrick White Fellowship. His most recent film is the French
language *In the Shadow of Iris*. Other films include
Edge of Darkness, *Blessed*, *The Fisherman's Wake*, *Piccolo Mondo*,
Strictly Ballroom and the multi-award-winning *Lantana*.

[Photo: Jeremy Shaw]

5 stars

Andrew Bovell

David and Margaret have always made me feel a little nervous. I think it's because they remind me of my parents. It's as though I expect David to ask me if I have done my homework and Margaret to tell me to change my shirt.

My father had that white grey hair that David has (as I do now). And he was occasionally prone to delivering a lecture if he felt there was a need for it. He could seem stern, even distant, and yet his eyes often betrayed a swell of emotion within, as I have seen David's eyes do. My mother was always battling with her hair trying to control it with a new style. And she was sassy and bold and liked a glass of white wine and said what she felt, like I have seen Margaret do.

I am not the first person to make the observation that their on-screen relationship is like that of a marriage. Their gentle teasing, their moments of tension and frustration with each other and their enduring fondness for one another is like two people who have been married for a long time. Dad died before *Lantana* came out but I can remember Mum phoning me excitedly from Perth to say that David and Margaret had given it five stars, the implication being that it must be all right then.

I wasn't convinced either, that *Lantana* would be a success until David and Margaret delivered their verdict on *The Movie Show*. Often their respective responses to films would be polarised, delivering scores at either end of the spectrum. If David went five, Margaret would go one and vice versa. Their difference in opinion was a part of the show's pleasure and success. And if they agreed at all, it was usually on films they judged to be average, both awarding it three stars. It was unusual for them to be in such strong agreement on a film they both liked.

I'd loved the film, of course, since I saw it evolve in the editing room, sitting alongside Ray Lawrence and Jan Chapman, and after wrestling with it as a screenplay for several years. I just wasn't sure that other people would feel the same way.

At the time Australians had become used to seeing themselves represented through the exaggerated lens of the decade's most successful films, *Strictly Ballroom* (1992), *Muriel's Wedding* (1994), *Priscilla, Queen of the Desert* (1994) and *The Castle* (1998). They were bright, comic and celebratory depictions of our suburban heritage. All four films had been extremely successful at the box office. And then a counterweight landed in the form of an atmospheric and serious relationship drama, shot in natural light, in hues of blue, depicting an urban and emotionally articulate set of characters navigating their way through the more serious issues of their lives. The predominant view of the time was that the audience wasn't interested in 'serious' films. *Lantana* was to prove that view wrong. But we didn't know that then. We had confidence in the artistic vision of the film. We just weren't sure if it would connect with an audience. Perhaps you never can be but there was nothing that preceded it that we could measure it against and no genre of Australian film that it could sit comfortably within. It broke new ground in how Australians depicted themselves in their cinema and we just weren't sure how the audience would respond.

Shortly before its Australian release, *Lantana* received a gala screening at the 2001 Toronto Film Festival. The day before terrorists had flown two planes into the World Trade Center towers in New York and the world had changed. Naturally, the Toronto audience was distracted and so it was difficult to get a read on the response to the film. For a moment film didn't matter all that much, even to the cinephiles gathered in Toronto. Margaret and David were there at the time and were caught up in the uncertainty.

As we built towards the film's release in early October, I was convinced that if people turned to cinema at all it would be to escape those dark times through comedy or fantasy or action films. What could this little film about love and marriage and trust and betrayal offer at such a time?

We opened modestly on twelve screens. The film had opened the Sydney Film Festival earlier in the year and had screened at the Melbourne Film Festival so there was some word of mouth and expectation. David and Margaret delivered their verdict to the public when *The Movie Show* screened two days after release. There was a steady build through the week and then the box office exploded on the weekend, with queues forming at many inner-city cinemas. Palace Cinemas rapidly built the number of screens to meet the demand – forty then eighty, then one hundred and twenty.

There's no doubt that Margaret and David's unequivocal endorsement contributed to the build in energy and anticipation around the film. I think it would have found its audience but it would have taken longer to do so and perhaps would have not been so broad without *The Movie Show*'s response, such was the reach of Margaret and David's audience and the respect with which their opinions were held.

They speak with great authority about film. It's an authority based on their shared knowledge and experience, of course – which is immense. But it is also based on their shared passion for cinema. When they review they are talking about something they love. Cinema matters to them, they argue about it because they care about it. It means something important to them and this is evident in the way they speak about it. It gives their respective voices great authenticity.

It is often said that while Margaret responds to a film with her heart, David responds with his head. And this balance is the secret of their success. This is true and yet so is its opposite. I have seen David respond with great emotion to a film just as I have seen Margaret respond with a sharp intellectual and critical eye. I think it is in the way they have been marketed that leads us to think that one is the head and one is the heart. But it is that each have both in equal measure that makes them who they are. There is no cynicism in their approach, as there often is with critics. They are driving no agenda except for the love of cinema as an art form that communicates what it means to be human and they are exemplary at the task of communicating this to an audience.

If they were the film and I was the critic I would have no choice but to award them five stars.

the 5-star films

2046 (2004)

21 Grams (2003)

A Separation (2011)

A Touch of Spice (2003)

All About My Mother (2000)

Amour (2012)

Apocalypse Now Redux (1979)

The Barbarian Invasions (2003)

The Battle of Algiers (1966)

Being John Malkovich (1999)

Big Night (1996)

The Big Sleep (1946)

Bowling For Columbine (2002)

Bright Star (2009)

Brokeback Mountain (2005)

Bulworth (1998)

The Butcher Boy (1997)

Calle 54 (2000)

Capote (2005)

Capturing The Friedmans (2003)

Chicago (2002)

The Child (2005)

The Circle (2000)

The Claim (2000)

The Conversation (1974)

The Cooler (2003)

The Corporation (2003)

Dancer in the Dark (2000)

Dave Chappelle's Block Party (2005)

Deconstructing Harry (1997)

Dogville (2003)

Drifting Clouds (1996)

E.T. the Extraterrestrial (1982)

Exile in Sarajevo (1997)

The Exorcist (1973)

Eyes Wide Shut (1999)

Facing the Music (2001)

Fargo (1996)

Fight Club (1999)

The Fog of War (2003)

The Godfather (1972)

Good Night, and Good Luck (2005)

Gran Torino (2008)

Grizzly Man (2005)

Hana-bi (1997)

Happy Feet (2006)

Hero (2002)

High Fidelity (2000)

Holy Smoke (1999)

The Hours (2002)

Hugo (2011)

Idiot Box (1996)

In the Cut (2003)

In the Mood for Love (2000)

The Incredibles (2004)

Into the Arms of Strangers (2000)

Into the Wild (2007)

It All Starts Today (1999)

The Italian (2005)

Kill Bill Vol. 1 (2003)

Kill Bill Vol. 2 (2004)
Kundun (1997)
Lantana (2001)
Last Days (2005)
Last Orders (2001)
Leaving Las Vegas (1995)
The Leopard (1963)
The Life Aquatic with Steve Zissou (2004)
The Lives of Others (2006)
The Lord of the Rings: The Fellowship of the Ring (2001)
The Lord of the Rings: The Return of the King (2003)
Lost in Translation (2003)
Lust, Caution (2007)
Master and Commander: The Far Side of the World (2003)
Melancholia (2011)
Metropolis (1927)
Milk (2008)
My Name is Joe (1998)
Mystic River (2003)
Nashville (1975)
The New World (2005)
Nil by Mouth (1997)
No Country for Old Men (1997)
North by Northwest (1959)
Not One Less (1999)
One Day in September (2000)
Paradise Now (2005)
The Pillow Book (1996)
The Portrait of a Lady (1996)

The Quiet Room (1996)
Rats in the Rank (1996)
Rear Window (1954)
The Road to Guantanamo (2006)
Romeo + Juliet (1996)
Russian Ark (2002)
Samson & Delilah (2009)
Shakespeare in Love (1998)
Shine (1996)
Sin City (2005)
The Social Network(2010)
Some Like it Hot (1959)
Talk to Her (2002)
Ten (2002)
There Will Be Blood (2007)
The Thin Red Line (1998)
The Third Man (1949)
The Three Burials of Melquiades Estrada (2005)
Tinker Tailor Soldier Spy (2011)
Touch of Evil (1958)
The Tree Of Life (2011)
The Truman Show (1998)
Turtles Can Fly (2004)
Ulysses' Gaze (1995)
Vertigo (1958)
War of the Worlds (2005)
The War Zone (1999)
When We Were Kings (1996)
The Wild Bunch (1969)
The Wrestler (2008)
Yi Yi (2000)

with thanks

Amanda Duthie
Director, Adelaide Film Festival

first met Margaret and David in the lifts at SBS TV, Milsons Point. I was young and working two jobs: by day the one-inch tape girl in the tape library, by night serving beer in Balmain. I learnt about the life cycle of production and broadcasting from wheeling around that now obsolete format ... inches and inches of stories on tape from around the world.

I would go home at night to tell my flatmates about the heady world of public broadcasting – and they just wanted to know if Margaret and David fought in the corridors as much as they did on the telly.

They didn't of course. But through them we were gifted the riches of world cinema, which sprang onto our screens and into our homes each week. They presented a degustation of cinematic delights. And they encouraged such good work – the women directors, the Indigenous screen creatives, and the important and the hidden and the taboo stories of Australia – and helped to take those films out into the world.

A review is a delicate thing; too much praise and people stop believing. Too much cynicism and people stop trusting. A critic has a responsibility to appreciate the massive human collective effort it takes to make a film – to understand it is no easy undertaking. That there is a broader industry machine behind these on-screen stories. That filmmakers are creating work for audiences who may not be in the image of the critic.

Margaret and David know the show-business and the screen-business. They recognise the creative spirit and they love film.

I am so pleased that they have been part of the Adelaide Film Festival, and that I met them all those years ago on my start in this industry. They introduced me to their so very lovely and very clever producer Richard Kuipers. I thank them most for that.

This book has been a pleasurable effort for so many brilliant people in the industry – filmmakers, festival makers, journalists and critics, friends and family.

Thanks to everyone for sharing. Thanks go to the Adelaide Film Festival team, especially Jane Howard. And a huge thanks and acknowledgment to Sandy George for shaping the tale of these two critics.

ANDREW BOVELL

The alchemy of collaboration

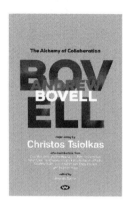

Christos Tsiolkas, Cate Blanchett, Andrew Upton, Patricia Cornelius, Tony Ayres, Jan Chapman, Lally Katz, Anthony LaPaglia, Geoffrey Rush, Chris Drummond, Eddie Perfect, Stephen Page

In *Andrew Bovell: The alchemy of collaboration*, Australian artists and filmmakers pay tribute to one of Australia's greatest writers for stage and screen. Andrew Bovell's credits include the landmark film *Lantana* and the award-winning play *When the Rain Stops Falling*. He adapted Kate Grenville's book *The Secret River* for stage and John le Carre's *A Most Wanted Man* for the big screen.

> 'The truth of the drama he writes carries equally well in a nine-hundred-seat theatre or in a close-up, because the truth is always at the heart of his work.'
> – Andrew Upton and Cate Blanchett

Wakefield Press is an independent publishing and
distribution company based in Adelaide, South Australia.
We love good stories and publish beautiful books.
To see our full range of books, please visit our website at
wakefieldpress.com.au
where all titles are available for purchase.

Find us!

Twitter: www.twitter.com/wakefieldpress
Facebook: www.facebook.com/wakefield.press
Instagram: instagram.com/wakefieldpress

Printed in Australia
AUOC02n1603011117
291096AU00011B/11/P